THE WISDOM OF JAMES

Word and Deed for the Diaspora

Ehud M. Garcia, Ph.D.

Copyright © 2008 by Ehud M. Garcia, Ph.D.

The Wisdom Of James: Word and Deed for the Diaspora
by Ehud M. Garcia, Ph.D.

Printed in the United States of America

ISBN 978-1-60647-914-8

All rights reserved solely by the author. The author guarantees all contents are original and do not infringe upon the legal rights of any other person or work. No part of this book may be reproduced in any form without the permission of the author. The views expressed in this book are not necessarily those of the publisher.

Unless otherwise indicated, Bible quotations are taken from The *Holy Bible, New International Version®,* Copyright © 1973, 1978, 1984 by International Bible Society. Used by permission of International Bible Society. *"NIV"* and *"New International Version"* are trademarks registered in the United States Patent and Trademark office by International Bible Society, and marked (ESV) are from The Holy Bible, English Standard Version, Copyright © 2001 by Crossway Bibles, a division of Good News Publishers, Used by permission, and marked (NKJV) are from The Holy Bible, New King James Version, Copyright © 1979, 1980, 1982 by Thomas Nelson, Inc., Used by permission, and marked (NSV) are from The Holy Bible, Revised Standard Version, Copyright © 1962 by The World Publishing Company, Used by permission.

www.xulonpress.com

Dedication

To Neiva, Esther and Gabriella

To Rubens Garcia

To Bob Holloway *(in memoriam)*

Preface

The idea for this book grew out of my preaching on it in three different churches, twice in the United States and once in my homeland, Brazil. Actually, the first time around was at the Inhumas Presbyterian Church, Brazil, some twenty-five years ago. I was a newly ordained pastor then and fresh out of seminary. During that time, I had a sense of urgency in trying to see everything done instantly; I mean, I wanted the church to change in a record pace. It is a dream most of us pastors have when we are first commissioned to the task. In my case, besides urgency, I was scared to death: My greatest fear was the fact that I really did not know what to do even though I had just finished seminary and was appointed as a professor of Hebrew and Old Testament in a newly formed seminary in my Presbytery.

What gave me the courage to preach a series in James was my desire to see the Word of God lived in the lives of everyone in the church, starting with me. Suddenly I realized that being out of seminary meant a new thing to me: "Reality." It was then that I realized that the Bible was more important than just a tool for ministry. I needed, more than ever, the precious teaching of the Gospel, but also I needed a new and fresh dosage of God's wisdom for the daily ministry that he had entrusted me. I knew that I needed that message from James. For quite some time I had been reading it and being challenged by the words that spoke so deeply to my spirit then (and still do today). Before then, I had had the experience of going through the first letter of John in another church and by doing so— through expository preaching—, I had the blessing of witnessing an entire congregation being transformed through a major act of reconciliation. That gave me an affirming sense that expounding James would be a blessing for both preacher and members of the church in Inhumas. And it sure was! In a matter of months, as I progressed in my exposition, I could see dramatic changes taking place in our lives. The same was true for the other two congregations in the United States.

Thus the major motivation for me to write this book has been the results of my preaching in James throughout the years. It has brought a positive note in my "portfolio," if I may use such analogy. On one occasion, I met a lady who was a member of one of the churches I served and she showed me notes of my preaching that she still uses on a regular basis. Granted, notes do not mean much sometimes: Sometimes I take notes of messages that I hear here and there and ten years from now I will probably find them somewhere. Not with this sister in Christ. She told me that she often goes back to those notes and studies them again and again. There are many cases of transformation that I would like to mention here. Without going in details, I have seen, as a result of this teaching, elders changing their business practices, people overcoming their prejudices, others going to the mission field. The list is long enough to have me convinced that the Word of God is powerful and effective when properly expounded. I pray that the Word of God will work its own power of transformation in the reader's life as an affirmation of God's wisdom.

James' purpose, according to this book, is to help the reader to realize his or her need for daily wisdom from God in order to go through life with the assurance that "the testing of your faith develops perseverance." But, if we do not ask God for wisdom, we will not get to the end of the day. He writes to his Church and to us that, "if any of [us] lacks wisdom, [we] should ask God who gives generously to all without finding fault, and it will be given to [us]" (1:5). He goes on to explain, through several key points in Christian life, the importance of acquiring wisdom in order to overcome the sometimes overwhelming challenges that we face in our walk with Jesus. There are two kinds of wisdom, one from above and the other from below, but only the wisdom that comes from God is the one that will illuminate and guide our walk of faith.

The *sine qua non* goal that James has in mind is that the followers of Jesus will walk in faith but also in deed. The Christian Faith is anchored in the Word of God but if we do not apply that Word in our lives, we will not practice our faith. Therefore, if we do not walk our talk, faith will be dead, totally barren. While we are totally, completely justified before God by faith, our faith will be justified before our fellow humans through the evidences of our faith. And here James is not shy in saying that it is our deeds that will justify us before those who are watching us. Thus, he points out that, "a person is justified by what he does and not by faith alone" (2:24). Here, at the same time that we are justified before God, we are also justified before humankind.

This book is for you and for me. Let us come to it with our open Bibles so we may see how closely is James following the Sermon on the Mount. Together we will grow in our humbleness before the Majesty of the Lord Jesus Christ. But we will be again compelled to practice the faith that once was given to us by the power of the Holy Spirit.

I want to thank God for the opportunity of writing this book. I thank him for the lessons I have learned as I went through the Epistle of James so many times, sometimes thinking that I was just too tired to read it once more; but realizing later that by doing so new insights would be added to my notes. I did considerable reading on James, learning from outstanding commentators and other scholars. But I wanted to have this book as a reflection that comes from a pilgrim's heart to another's. Being an academician myself, I was tempted to make this book an academic treatise; but this is not the goal that I purposed in my heart. I hope it will speak to all my friends in a way that is more conversational. I added a brief bibliography at the end for your further studies; but I did not put any reference when I quoted some of them, except that I mentioned the source by name.

I also want to thank my wife, Neiva, and my two daughters, Esther and Gabriella, for giving of their time while I spent numerous hours around this project. They have been a wonderful source of support and blessing to me during the time of this writing. I dedicate this book to them and to two other people who are important in the visualization and production of this project. My Dad, Rubens

Garcia, has been a great inspiration for me in the preparation of this book; he is one of the few people I have encountered who lives what James expects us to do in his Epistle. The example of his life has been the key factor in my conversion back to Christ when I was twenty-two years-old. He is my silent "Billy Graham." I want to also dedicate this book to a friend who has gone to be with the Lord just a few weeks ago. Bob Holloway was a man who inspired me to take courage and start writing with a definite sense of purpose; his life—we called him "Intrepid Bob"—was filled with great accomplishments and I had the great pleasure of being counted as one of his friends.

This is not a unique book; I am not here reinventing the wheel, so to speak. It is a collection of thoughts and illustrations around a topic that have so much wisdom shared by many good people. I relied a lot on John Calvin and Simon Kistemaker, for example. I am not afraid to say that I may have drawn some of my conclusions from numerous sources that I even do not remember anymore; being reading on James for so many years, my mind may have absorbed thoughts of precious brothers and sisters that I may have forgotten to give them the proper credit. I apologize for that upfront and welcome any comment and suggestion leading me to make the needed corrections and giving necessary credits in the future.

The challenge of writing a book in English was the most daring to me. English is my second language and I am still learning it after more than thirty years of daily use of this beautiful language. Only a fool would dare to write in a second or third language; so, allow me to include myself among them. But I feel more comfortable writing in this wonderful language than in my native one, Portuguese. Half of my life has been already in North America and I feel that, by being bi-cultural, I should try to write in English at least once. So here I am: writing a book in English! When I wrote my doctoral dissertation, I had to add a disclaimer at the very beginning of my thesis, because it was written in a language other than my mother tongue. The same I do here in this paragraph. Not only do I have a spoken accent, I still hold a lot of my Portuguese grammatical structures when I write in English or in Spanish. I decided to leave it this

The Wisdom Of James

way for a simple reason: I would like to have you experience what is in my heart when I write.

Soli Deo Gloria!

Lewiston, Idaho
9 September 2008

Table Of Contents

Preface vii

1. Reaching for the Diaspora – 1:1 15
2. The Pure and Faultless Religion – 1:27 27
3. The Testing of Our Faith – 1:2-4 39
4. Asking for Wisdom – 1:5-8 49
5. Trials and Temptations – 1:2-18 59
6. Doers of the Word – 1:19-27 69
7. Faith and Law: The Test of Love – 2:1-13 79
8. Faith and Deeds: The Test of Orthodoxy – 2:14-26 91
9. The Use of the Tongue: The Test of Maturity – 3:1-12 ... 105
10. Two Kinds of Wisdom: Handling Them Wisely – 3:13-18 115
11. Asking With the Wrong Motives: The Test of Prayer – 4:1-3 125

The Wisdom Of James

12. The Secret of Walking With God: The Test of
    Humility – 4:4-12 137

13. Deo Volente! Submission to God's Will – 4:13-17 149

14. Impatience Toward the Rich: The Test of
    Justice – 5:1-6 161

15. Waiting for Deliverance: The Test of
    Patience – 5:7-12 175

16. Earnest Prayer: The Test of Mutuality – 5:13-18 185

17. Rescuing the Wayward: The Test of
    Forgiveness – 5:19-20 197

Chapter 1

Reaching for the Diaspora

James 1:1

To write about the Epistle of James through a series of messages is a difficult task. I believe, however, it is part of a great privilege for a pastor who, like me, finds himself in the Christian Diaspora. It challenges me to open my heart to the fact of being a pilgrim and at the same time a shepherd of a flock that the Holy Spirit has put under my responsibility. Before I move on, I want to make sure that I hear what the Lord has to say to me as a follower of Jesus Christ; as a pastor, I am also under the care of the Great Shepherd. I need this teaching more than anybody else.

This chapter is a brief introduction of the entire letter; it will cover important introductory issues such as format, authorship, date, and audience. It will also bring forth the overall idea of the epistle, showing us some key topics that James wanted to convey to the dispersed people of God, beginning with the members of the Church in Jerusalem, which were being forced out of the City of Gold into the *Diaspora*. As I present some elements of James, I want to emphasize again the center of his message: He wants to describe the True Religion; that is, the Christian Religion. More on that will be covered in the next chapter. As he tries to accomplish his goal, James deals with the Wisdom from Above, the Wisdom of God. He

The Wisdom Of James

reflects very closely the teachings of Jesus Christ during his earthly ministry. We will see more on that as we explore his teachings.

Who Wrote the Epistle of James?

We learn from the very outset that James was a "servant of God and of the Lord Jesus Christ." That is all he has to say about himself. James was a disciple of Jesus Christ and wanted to introduce himself on the basis of his own faith. As such, he established his spiritual relationship with the Jesus Christ; not his physical relationship with the Lord. As we will learn below, he had the unique opportunity to use his brother, the Lord Jesus Christ, as a personal influence that would make him part of any inner circle in his time. Usually we have the tendency of appropriating some influential things in our lives to make us feel important; even more powerful. Contrary to the normal and expected idea, James did not take advantage of his family relationship with the Lord Jesus; instead, he introduces himself as being a simple bond slave of God and his Master and his Lord, Jesus Christ.

This creates a problem when we want to establish the authorship of the Epistle. There are other Jameses that are mentioned in the New Testament; and, at the first sight, any one could have been a good candidate to be the author of this Epistle. Nevertheless, we will see that there is only one possible author, and that is James, the son of Mary and Joseph, the brother of Jesus of Nazareth.

Among the several possible names, we will attain to the most evident in the New Testament. The first of them is "James the son of Zebedee." He was the brother of John. The two brothers were also called *Boanerges*, which means "sons of Thunder" (Mark 3:17). He was named among the Twelve Disciples and also included in the inner circle of Jesus; often named along with his brother John and Peter. Not much is said about him, however. We do not find a great deal about him, except that he was one of the Twelve Apostles. James was decapitated by the order of King Herod Agrippa I in A.D. 44 (Acts 12:2). The date of his death is prior to the earliest possible date for the writing of the Epistle of James. Therefore, we may say conclusively that he could not have been the author of the Epistle.

The Wisdom Of James

Another James is named in the New Testament: "James the son of Alphaeus." He was also one of the apostles, but we don't know anything about him, except that he was listed among the Twelve. If he were the author of the Epistle, certainly he would have given more details about himself in the introduction of the letter. Yet another James appears in the time of Jesus: "James the Younger." According to Mark 15:40, "Some women were watching from a distance. Among them were Mary Magdalene, Mary the mother of James the younger and of Joses, and Salome." Being identified as James the younger; his mother is probably the wife of Clopas (John 19:25). None of these two could have been the author of the Epistle of James.

There is one left, who is without any doubt the author of the Epistle: James, the pastor of the Church of Jerusalem. He is the only one who fits the characteristics of the author of this Epistle is James. He was the [half] brother of Jesus Christ. James was born after Jesus Christ. Therefore, he was conceived as an offspring of Joseph and Mary. We are reminded that Jesus was conceived by the Holy Spirit, being born to Mary before she had any sexual relationship with her husband Joseph. That is why some commentators, among them Simon Kistemaker, prefer to call James a half brother of Jesus. There is enough evidence to suggest that he was the oldest of the brothers and sisters of Jesus. He did not need any further introduction in the Epistle, everyone would have recognized him immediately because of his strong leadership in the Church of Jerusalem. Although he was not a believer before Jesus' resurrection (John 7:5), he came to faith when Jesus appeared to him after his resurrection (1 Corinthians 15:7). Paul speaks of him thrice in Galatians (1:19; 2:9, 12). James was the one who spoke most fluently in the first assembly in Jerusalem, and he was the one who wrote the letter to be read to all Gentile churches after that cross-cultural related assembly (Acts 15:13). Later he met Paul when the Apostle to the Gentiles gave his report back in Jerusalem (Acts 21:18).

James, the brother of Jesus Christ, was a faithful servant of God Almighty and of the Lord Jesus Christ. He made clear his confession of faith. Although he could have used his brotherly relationship with the Lord Jesus, he knew that his relationship with his brother was deeper than any physical connection they had. An important lesson we learn from this: No one will be saved by physical descent; only through faith in the saving work of the Lord Jesus Christ.

What is the Format of the Epistle of James?

Is it a letter or an epistle? It is an Epistle: it has the addressee, but it is not bound to any specific date; that is, it is timeless in its message. Different from a letter, it does not have a final salutation. We may use, however, the two terminologies interchangeably; most of the students of this Epistle use the two terms in that way. For consistency reasons, I will try to use the term "Epistle" more often.

It was written in a very good Greek, which raises a problem for some scholars to accept James, Jesus' brother, as the author. He grew up in Galilee, son of a simple carpenter, and yet, he wrote in a most beautiful Greek. However, there are at least two points in favor of his authorship: First, he grew up in an environment where Greek was predominant, not Hebrew or Aramaic. Therefore, he was well acquainted with the language. Second, although the Greek is very good, there is a number of "Hebraisms" in the Epistle. It is like someone who knows a lot of a second language but his or her cultural values, worldview, and first language idioms, and so on, seem to interfere in the flow of the second language she or he is speaking or writing. I am an example of that: I was born and raised in Brazil. My mother tongue is Portuguese. But my wife and I moved to North America in 1984 where we live up to this date. We became bicultural persons and also dual citizens. By normal standards, my fluency in English is very good, but when I speak or write, I still have an accent and also many of my sentences and lines of thought follow the Portuguese structure. The same happens in James: He was a bicultural person, spoke at least three different languages. Although he spoke and wrote Greek fluently, he grew up in a Jewish Family and was taught from early childhood the Hebrew Bible, along with all the cultural worldview of the Old Testament. In fact, James writes like an Old Testament Prophet in many ways. The tone of his teaching is prophetic and full of admonitions.

The Wisdom Of James

From an historical view, the Epistle deals with a number of problems that had been occurring among the people who were under James' leadership and also in other areas where the Church of Jesus Christ was present. It is a document that fits the paraenetic literature. Let me explain, even so briefly. The Epistle of James forms a set of ethic and moral instructions, most commonly understood as *paraenesis* among theologians, ethicists and exegetes. The term comes from the Latin and brings the idea of giving advice or exhortation. Thus, the purpose of James is to admonish the Church and instruct its members about serious problems that were present in his time; and, more than ever, in our present day too. Let me try to build the possible situation for James in words that will capture his moment: James had become the leader in the Jerusalem Church. As a result of that, he became aware of numerous new situations that were coming to the fore, good and bad, not only in Jerusalem but also all over the place. I can only imagine how he collected the topics for his writing: maybe he had a short list of situations that was growing; but he did not have the need to organize them in any kind of sequence or literary form. His concern was to address those issues, probably as they came to him in order of need. His taxonomy does not necessary follow the consensus of any literary organization as some scholars have realized. In my own experience, I have noticed that when I have to address issues that must be dealt with, I will sometimes deal with them as a first-come-first-serve priority. I think, James dealt with those issues in that matter and as he went along, he sometimes would come back to something he had made mention before. An example of this is when he mentions the problem with the tongue in 1:26 and then writes more extensively in chapter 3 — as a matter of fact, James makes reference to the tongue and its problems in more passages than we first realize: 1:26; 3:1-12; 4:11, 16; 5:9, 12 and probably in 2:6a-7. I think he was addressing some very important ethical and moral issues that are not only pertaining to his own situation but also are part of the universal moral principles that are present in the entire Scripture, including the teachings of Jesus Christ in the Sermon on the Mount, for example.

I like the way Leo G. Perdue defines *Paraenesis*. For him it is "a means by which an individual is introduced to the group's or role's social knowledge, including especially norms and values pertaining to group or role behavior, internalizes this knowledge, and makes it the basis for both behavior and the meaning system by which he interprets and orders his world." This definition will help us in some important areas of application of the Gospel in our lives. Here we see two dimensions of what the Bible is intended for our lives: first, it has the behavioral sense, which is closely linked with our cultural apparatus. All of us have grown up with a worldview that is intrinsically rooted in our cultural and societal values. The Word of God has the power of changing those worldviews for the good of the Kingdom of God. That is to say: the Gospel will change one's worldview in such a way that that person will commence a new life with the Lord showing new values that were not present before. Even those persons who had lived upright lives will show that their new values are higher that those they honestly honored before. The other aspect of this change is the core of James' effort in his Epistle: he is concerned with both Word and Deed. In fact, we come now to a key element in the Christian life. It is James' intention that those who read about what the "royal law found in Scripture" teaches be real practitioners of what they learned; in other words, they should practice their faith according to the teachings of the Gospel.

Even so, I think that James has a theological significance and bears an orderly sequence of thoughts that make it a whole. Rather than showing no apparent unity, it is an epistle that is divided in basically two long sermons. The first one cover chapters 1 and 2 and has fifty-three verses. The second covers the other three chapters and has fifty-five verses. It was written to be read to the churches of the Diaspora as sermons from their pastor: Pastor James of "the First Christian Church in Jerusalem."

As such, I follow the idea that this book is also an attempt to provide pastoral reflection for the reader. I believe that one of the key elements of James' theological intention is the testing of our faith in several ways. We are sojourners in a most intricate pilgrimage and this requires from us a certain level of spiritual maturity that will keep us *en route* to heaven, to our new country, to the New Jerusalem. In knowing this, we sometimes are overwhelmed by the trials and temptations that are so very often posed before us. The Christian

The Wisdom Of James

Life is full of trials and tribulations (John 16:33; Romans 8:28-39, 1 Peter 1:3-12), but we will be found "more than conquerors" through Christ. I chose my personal outline for the Epistle and made it into part of the outline of this book. As you will notice, every chapter deals with the test of our faith in various manners. I believe that they represent what my pastoral heart sees as the result of my pilgrimage, but also as the result of what I have experienced in my ministry in four different countries over the past twenty-five years.

To Whom was the Epistle Intended?

The opening of the Epistle is evident: "To the twelve tribes scattered among the nations." Who are they, then? They are members of the Church in Jerusalem who were scattered around the known world of that time. Both James and Peter called it the Diaspora, or Dispersion. The term *Diaspora* has been used for the Jewish people spread around the world. The same idea is also used today for different groups, religious, political, or even ethnic, in different places around the globe. For example, we may talk about the Hindus of the Indian Diaspora in Toronto, Canada. We may talk about the Chilean Diaspora, those who, because of their political views, had to flee Chile during the military takeover by Augusto Pinochet. Most of them live in three predominant places in the world: Spain, France, and Canada. We may also talk about the Japanese Diaspora, millions of Japanese people who migrated to Brazil. Back to James, in our case, the Diaspora was predominantly the Jewish Christian believers who were primarily members of the Church in Jerusalem; in Peter's case, it was the entire Church of Jesus spread around the world. I believe that today, both the Epistles of James and of Peter are to be read among the Christian Diaspora churches around the world until the Lord Jesus comes back again. In that case, we are as part of the audience of this Epistle as the first readers were.

It is, therefore, a universal epistle; that is, it is intended to be read in all churches until the Lord comes again. The Holy Spirit inspired it and his intention for the Epistle is to instruct the whole Body of Christ, the Church, throughout the centuries. Again, this is a very important portion of the New Testament Canon for today.

Unless we understand that this is probably the first body of the New Testament literature, written sometime between A.D. 46 and A.D. 62, when James died, we will not understand its context and contents. At the time of his writing, none of the Gospels had been written yet. Therefore, it was clearly written with the Jewish Christian Faith in mind; there were not many Gentile churches yet and, of course, James was concerned about the members of the Jerusalem Church, which was predominantly Jewish. This is something we must keep in mind. We cannot ask this Epistle to offer themes that are well demonstrated in the four Gospels, neither something that we may find of crucial importance in the Pauline Corpus. James wrote from what he had heard from Jesus Christ and from his teachings. We may suggest that James is in perfect harmony with Jesus' preaching, mainly the Sermon on the Mount. In fact, a number of the topics of the Epistle resemble that as we will see in the coming chapters.

What is the Message of James?

Before I present the content of James' message, it will help us to take a look on the purpose of the letter again. This is a pastoral letter and has the goal of providing a sense of pastoral care for those who are in the diaspora. James, as the leader of the Jerusalem Church, had to deal with numerous situations in that church; but at the same time, there is also the other side of the possible interest of James in regrouping the scattered church that had gone to the various parts of the then known world, mostly around the Mediterranean Sea.

An interesting approach to the structure and the purpose of this epistle comes from Timothy B. Cargal. He deals with the issue from a structural exegetical perspective (using structural semiotics), applying "'inverted parallelisms' between the opening (Jas 1:1) and closing (5:19-20) of the letter." It is his contention that James' main purpose was to restore those in the Diaspora who had gone astray. By that he uses the very first verse and the very last ones to validate his thesis, where he establishes the connection between the "twelve tribes of the Diaspora" (cf. 1:1) and then to restore those who have left the truth (cf. 5:19-20). At this point, it is not clear

The Wisdom Of James

for me, however, if James is dealing with those who departed from the Christian Faith, or simply from the Jewish Faith. To this point, I think it might create a situation in which either James is dealing with the already members of the Church or was he concerned with the Jewish brothers and sisters who had not yet come to the saving knowledge of Jesus Christ? There are some scholars who tend to maintain that James was writing primarily to the plain Jewish audience. This is not my position, as I have posted elsewhere.

As I mentioned before, the Epistle of James is a set of two sermons. But it has some important sub-points that will help us grow in our faith. We would dare to say, along with others, that the Epistle of James depicts the idea that "a living faith is a working faith." Much of the letter deals with key moral issues, not much with the theological issues of the life, death, resurrection, and ascension of Jesus. James was a practical person and he wanted his church to be obedient to the Law of Love; that is, the Law of Jesus Christ. In that matter, he did not have much time to go into the philosophical aspects of faith. The Holy Spirit was going to use others (Matthew, Mark, Luke, John, Paul, and Peter) to do that. But James was the "hands-on" person. He dealt with the practical side of the Faith; that is, with the application of the Great Commandment of Jesus Christ (Matthew 22:37-37; cf. James 2:1-13).

Even though I see James as a practical person, I tend to join the crowd and suppose that we may be tempted to suggest that there is not much theology in his Epistle. We will find out, however, that the author had a keen theological view of faith; the only thing is that he saw it from a practical way. We may suggest that James is an excellent book on practical theology. It is as valuable in that area as the Pastoral Letters from Paul. The difference is that here he is instructing the Church as a Body; in Paul's case, he is instructing two of his disciples, Timothy and Titus. As mentioned before, James drew his theological framework from Jesus Christ's preaching and teaching, mostly from the Sermon on the Mount and other teachings that the Master had passed on to him. His theology complements the core of Paul's teaching on faith, for example — better said: Paul's theology, which came to us much later, complements James' views on faith. Although Luther considered this Epistle to be spurious, calling it "an epistle of straw," we see that the Holy Spirit used James to show what Faith is in practical terms. We will explore this more closely when we study the second chapter of the Epistle, when James and Paul used the same illustration of Abraham, but provided two complementing conclusions for that.

We can divide the Epistle into several different themes. In fact, I would like to invite you to do that: take time and read the Epistle several times. After you get really acquainted with its message as a whole, take time and write down the many topics that you find in that book. After doing that, try to build your own outline of the Epistle. You will learn a lot by doing that. You will be surprised by the fact that there is a wealth of teachings that might pop up right in front of your eyes. In the meantime, I would like to suggest the following basic important themes that we may explore by taking each chapter as a whole:

1. 1:1-27 — Perseverance
2. 2:1-26 — Faith
3. 3:1-18 — Restraint
4. 4:1-17 — Submission
5. 5:1-20 — Patience

As mentioned before, we will be able to realize that there are several sub-themes in the Epistle and the coming chapters will deal with them. In fact, the Epistle of James is rich in all aspects; it is a great blessing for those who are in a pilgrimage, looking forward to the complete realization of the Kingdom of God.

In view of the above, what to expect from the study of James? There is a lot to be said about it, but the most important thing to point out is that I believe this book will transform our views on Faith and will enable us to worship God with a new vision of who he is and how we should offer our lives to him on a daily basis. Borrowing from Paul to the Romans, how to offer up ourselves as a living sacrifice to the one who is worthy of all praises and honor and glory forever. We will deal with some hard issues in this study. I am confident that it will bring forth the many blessings that the Lord has stored for you.

The Wisdom Of James

You will learn that the Lord is there for you all the time; he is in control of our lives and nothing will escape his loving care for us and also for those he is calling into a new relationship with him. As we will see, the Lord is full of compassion and mercy. Because of that, we may say with confidence that he wants the best for us, even though he allows us to go through trials and tribulations.

You will also learn that the Lord admonishes his people in order to bring them to the realization that he disciplines those whom he loves the most: his children. You are part of his family and because of that you are growing up spiritually to become a mature Christian. It is the purpose of God to change us into the image of Jesus Christ. We were predestined to be conformed to the image of the Son of God (Romans 8:29-30), and this will be attained by a life that will show spiritual maturity over the years.

You will learn that the process of growing up in your spiritual life takes time and a lot of perseverance. I prefer the term "patience," however. But do not be discouraged, the Lord will help you through that process; he is faithful.

Chapter 2

The Pure and Faultless Religion

James 1:27

I would like to start with a quote from a Presbyterian minister from the Seventeenth Century, William Sprague. In dealing with revival, he provided a definition of religion that I believe fits well with the Epistle of James' central theme: the True Religion. The following quote is simple and to the point: "Religion consists in the conformity of the heart and life with the will of God." I suggest that the Epistle of James is of great necessity for us today because it deals with Religion.

We live in a time where spirituality is in the rise; there are thousands of different religions in the world and, not only us, but our neighbors are also confused on how to explain the contemporary religious phenomenon. A few years ago, a news piece on the public television showed a woman who had merged no less than thirteen different religions into her personal view of spirituality. Her view of religion was primarily something that initiated in her and that she had full control of. In her mind, the more religions she incorporated into her personal Pantheon, the more she was free to worship whomever, or whatever, she wanted. It was sad to see her so proudly telling the reporter about her religious preference; but at the same time, it was a small demonstration of what human beings are prone to do. That news page reminded me of Paul's teaching

to the Romans about the profile of the person who has intention-
ally rejected the Lord Almighty. That was a portrait of an ungodly,
unrighteous person whose picture is well presented in Romans 1:18-
3:19. It is a dramatic description of the fallen human race that so
despairingly need the Lord Jesus Christ as the only Redeemer in
their lives. I must add that this is the picture of any person who does
not have the gift of Salvation yet. We cannot forget that before we
came to know Jesus Christ, we all were dead in our trespasses and
we were under the dominion of Satan (Ephesians 2:1-5). It is imperative that we grasp this truth at this stage so others will not state
that Christians are superior than others. The matter of being saved
is more humbling than we can imagine; it is because of God's grace
and mercy that we were chosen before the foundation of the world.
God did not take any good or bad in our future lives as a condition for election; he chose his children when we were totally dead
spiritually, and nothing that he had foreseen in us contributed to his
choosing us. This is the great meaning of grace! And at the same
time, we should be forever grateful to the Lord for being chosen
to receive eternal life; otherwise we would probably be doing even
worse things, worshiping all kinds of idols and false gods, and so
forth.

What Is a Pure and Faultless Religion?

The question then comes to us: What is the True Religion? James
brings some key answers for that persistent question. A brief look
on the text will help us to set the tone for our understanding of this
chapter. Before I move on, I would like to discuss some important
terms in this text of James. As I do so, I want to emphasize that
this passage is the key verse for the entire Epistle. Everything that
he wrote is related to the pure and faultless religion, which is the
Christian Faith.

Religion

The first term I would like to introduce is the word *Religion*. I
should take two approaches to the origin of this word in order to

The Wisdom Of James

better understand it in the context of James. First, the word *Religion* originates from the Latin. There are two possibilities for its formation. It could be *relego* or *religo*. The former is derived from *re* and *legere*, meaning "to read over again." The latter comes from the composition of *re* and *ligare*, meaning "to bind back." It gives the idea of reconnecting; in the biblical sense, it should be understood as what Paul teaches in his writings about *reconciliation* (Romans 5:1-10; 2 Corinthians 5:11-21). In once sense, Religion started exactly where and when humankind lost fellowship or communion with God: at the Garden of Eden. As soon as Adam and Eve fell in disobedience, their communion with God was broken. They came to the realization that their disobedience created a breach in their relationship with the Creator and thus they tried to rebuild that relationship by their own efforts. We learn in Genesis that they tried to cover their iniquity using what they thought would cover their shame. But the Lord did not accept that as part of the reconciliation. Only later did God cover their shame by shedding the blood of animals and using their skin to cover them, "The LORD God made garments of skin for Adam and his wife and clothed them" (Genesis 3:21). Adam's and Eve's attempt to rebuild their communion with God translates well the meaning of Religion, which is the attempt to reconnect or to bind back.

But the Greek word in James bears a different meaning. The word is *threeskeia*, also found in Acts 26:5 and Colossians 2:18, meaning the external service of worship. In fact, the term *Religion* has been consistently used as an Elizabethan English word to "denote the outward expression of worship." Here we find a difference between Religion and Godliness, which is important for our understanding of the Epistle of James. Being an outward expression of worship, Religion must go beyond the mere ritualism of Judaism. Godliness, as we know in the Bible, is an internal service; we might, therefore, compare it with the "soul of worship." James repudiated the ritualism of the Jewish faith; therefore, he wanted his flock to demonstrate their inner faith through a religion that was true and undefiled. That is the center of his concerns for the religious life of his people. Of course, the climax of his teaching on this matter comes from James 2:17, where we learn that faith without work is dead.

The Wisdom Of James

Pure

The next term that invites a brief description is the word *Pure*. It can be translated as "pure," "truthful," "sincere," and "genuine." The Greek word is *kathara* (nominative form of *katharos*) and appears seven times in the New Testament. Twice in the Gospels, the first is found in Matthew 27:59, when Joseph of Arimathea, a wealthy disciple of Jesus, provided the means for the Lord's burial. The text reads that he wrapped the Lord in "clean linen cloth." The second is found in Luke 11:41, when Jesus denounces the Pharisees and the Lawyers, when they asked why the disciples did not wash their hands before eating. Jesus answered them properly and added that, "everything will be clean to you." Paul uses this word four times: Romans 14:20; 1 Timothy 3:9; 2 Timothy 1:3, and Titus 1:5. The translation of the work is both "clean" and "pure." And the seventh use of the word is in James, which is found in the present text we are reading.

It is appropriate to introduce two verses that are related to what James wants to convey. The first is found in Isaiah, when the Lord is calling his people to reason with him. We read, "Wash yourselves; make yourselves clean; remove the evil of your doings from before my eyes; cease to do evil, learn to do good; seek justice, correct oppression; defend the fatherless, plead for the widow" (Isaiah 1:16-17, ESV). The second is taken from the Sermon on the Mount. Jesus introduces the sermon with the Beatitudes and one of them reads, "Blessed are the pure in heart, for they shall see God" (Matthew 5:8, ESV). These two passages show that the purity of the true religion must come from within, not from a mere external demonstration of religiosity. The well of purity is the heart of the person; therefore, James is calling his audience to consider the origination of their devotion to God.

Faultless

This next term can be also translated as "pure," "undefiled," and "unstained." The Greek word is *amiantos*. We find two other significant verses in which this adjective is used in this form, both

30

in the Letter to the Hebrews. The first talks about Jesus Christ as our High Priest and that he is "undefiled" (Hebrews 7:26); the second, Hebrews 13:4, deals with the sanctity of marriage and teaches us that in the Christian marriage, "marriage is honourable in all, and the bed undefiled" (KJV), that "marriage should be honored by all, and the marriage bed kept pure" (NIV). Here we seem to find a Hebraism in which James is emphasizing the purity of Religion. He uses two synonyms for pure, clean, undefiled, or unstained. But I think he wants to also emphasize something else: the need to have total freedom for worship, and that freedom comes from a clean heart. It reminds us of Psalm 24 where we read about those who will enter the presence of the Lord. The quote of the verse will explain my thought by itself: "Who shall ascend the hill of the LORD? He who has clean hands and a pure heart, who does not lift up his soul to what is false and does not swear deceitfully" (Psalm 24:3-4, ESV). Paul also has the same teaching when he talks about prayer, "I want men everywhere to lift up holy hands in prayer, without anger or disputing" (1 Timothy 2:8).

I also want to remind ourselves again that this word is used against the Jews who lived their lives in hypocrisy. They lived only ceremonial lives, observing external characteristics of their religion, according to their own desires (see verse 14). Because of that, Jesus used very hard words to them, as we can find in Matthew 23:23, "Woe to you, scribes and Pharisees, hypocrites! for you tithe mint and dill and cummin, and have neglected the weightier matters of the law, justice and mercy and faith; these you ought to have done, without neglecting the others" (RSV). In that line, another illustration comes from the hypocritical way in which the leaders of the Jews dealt with Jesus Christ during his trial. They did not want to be defiled in order to eat the Passover; therefore, they had to act swiftly. This is how John narrates the situation, "Then they led Jesus from the house of Caiaphas to the Praetorium. It was early. They themselves did not enter the Praetorium, so that they might not be defiled, but might eat the Passover" (John 18:28, RSV). This depicts the reason why James did not want his flock to be like the Judaic worshipers, whose cultus was merely external and void of any sincerity and meaning.

The Wisdom Of James

Just by looking at these few words in the text, we have before us a great opportunity to evaluate our spiritual journey with the Lord Jesus Christ. This is a great opportunity for us to know what is the pure religion that God accepts from his children. Therefore, we should move on to the core of the True Religion that our Lord God and Savior Jesus Christ accepts. What are the key elements of the Pure and Faultless Religion? I submit that there are at least three important ones: First, It is for our Triune God only; secondly, It exercises love for our neighbors; and thirdly, It is sanctified by God.

For Our Triune God Only

The text reads that "Religion that God our Father accepts..." This is an indication of how we should direct our worship to the Lord. The Jews thought that their morality, their moral life, was enough; but our religious life must be found *before* the Lord: "Religion that is pure and undefiled *before* God and the Father is this..." (RSV): Everything must be done for the glory of God! There is purpose in worship; it is not to be taken lightly. Worship demands an attitude of great submission to God; but also, it demands the certainty of who he is and why we are in his presence. We must be aware that when we prostrate ourselves before the Lord in worship, we are doing so for him, and him alone. Far from being critical, I have sometimes a hard time watching people worshiping either themselves or performing for others. I am not talking about a worship team in front of the people — although some do it for their own pleasure at times — but people who are trying to obtain the approval of those who are surrounding them. I remember being in a Pentecostal church in Recife, Brazil, years ago and observing a young man trying to convince others that he was speaking in tongues. He would speak the loudest and at the same time look around to see if the others, including myself, would pay any attention to him. When we are before the Lord we must come to him with all humbleness and submission; with fear and trembling because he is holy.

God does not share his glory with other gods. From the beginning he makes sure to us that he is the One and Only God. We read in Deuteronomy the command of the Lord to preserve the knowledge of him and pass that knowledge to our next generation. But he starts by telling the people and commanding them to, "Hear, O Israel: The LORD our God is one LORD! (Deuteronomy 6:4). The Ten Commandments destroy any doubt on this important issue: "You shall have no other gods before me" (Exodus 20:3). Our worship and obedience is to him only. This was key in the Apostles' confession of faith and practice. A great example of this is taken from the lives of Peter and John. According to Luke's narrative, we learn that "Peter and John replied, 'Judge for yourselves whether it is right in God's sight to obey you rather than God. For we cannot help speaking about what we have seen and heard'" (Acts 4:19-20).

This is serious business! We are in the presence of God Almighty when we are in worship. Worship is not a theatrical performance; it is not a form of gathering whose primary goal is to please ourselves. Rather, it is a time when we gather before the Lord to offer him what he is worth. To him and to him only belongs all the glory! Therefore, all glory must be returned to God: "For from him and through him and to him are all things. To him be glory for ever. Amen!" (Romans 11:36).

It Exercises Love to Our Neighbors

The text continues on to inform and to lead us "to look after orphans and widows in their distress..." This demonstrates the horizontal dimension of Christ's Law. If the primary attitude of our worship is towards God; the second is towards our neighbor. James capitalizes on this truth for the entire Epistle. He keeps in his mind the Great Commandment that Jesus Christ gave his disciples, the Law of Christ, as he put in Matthew, "Love the Lord your God with all your heart and with all your soul and with all your mind. . . . Love your neighbor as yourself." Our Lord Jesus concludes by saying that, "All the Law and the Prophets hang on these two commandments" (Matthew 22:37-40).

There is a *social dimension* in practicing our religion. God planned a way in which others will see how we show our faith to the world. Among many of the stories and parables that the Lord has taught James, we certainly are safe in mentioning the story of the Good Samaritan. If there is a story more compelling than that one for our days, we must find it soon. In fact, we live in a time when it has become more and more difficult to be a good Samaritan to our neighbors. We live in a time that has been plagued by fear and lack of mutual trust. On top of that, we seem to be brainwashed with the idea that we must live our lives in a most individualist way; help is something superficial, leading to nothing significant or transformational. We hear of great deeds done by many; groups of people travel distances to provide relief, but they leave, they don't stay. It is a quick form of involvement; it is a circumstantial necessity. Even so, only few are the good Samaritans in our days.

James will follow this line of argument in the second chapter as he presents his argument that faith without works is dead. We learn from other passages the same idea of True Religion. John explores it as well, "If anyone has material possessions and sees his brother in need but has no pity on him, how can the love of God be in him?" (1 John 3:17). Paul, in another occasion, wrote to the Church in Galatia to "bear one another's burdens, and so fulfill the law of Christ." (Galatians 6:2).

In this passage, God is not excluding the many people with their specific needs; here he brings to our attention the orphans and the widows because they were the most needy and vulnerable ones in the Early Church. The members of James' Church in Jerusalem who had been dispersed around the world were already under fierce persecution (see, for instance, Acts 6:1-5); many husbands and fathers had died because of their faith. But also, many orphans and widows had become followers of Jesus Christ and no longer were receiving welfare help from the Jewish Temple. They were in dire straits; they were the most fragile and powerless people under the care of the Church. Those outside the Church, however, were coming to them and the provision of help certainly was a way of evangelizing the new comers.

Kistemaker provides a good definition of those who follow the True Religion by helping the needy and downtrodden. He puts it this way, "the person who exhibits true religion visits the 'orphans and widows in their distress.' He puts his heart into being a guardian and provider, he alleviates their needs, and shows them the love of the Lord in word and deed (Matt. 25:35-40)."

Today, we may include the hungry, the homeless, the abandoned and lonely, the elderly without any proper care. Also we may include those who are hurting inside, who are suffering from spiritual, social and physical diseases that our age has produced: the lonely people, the suicidal teenagers, the drug addicted, and so forth. The term "to Look after" (NIV) or "to visit" (RSV) means more than just to go to someone's home for a chat and a cup of coffee. It means to minister through acts of love and mercy, to provide spiritual help and comfort. It means to bring the good news of salvation to those who are in desperate need: through counseling, reading the Scriptures, singing a song, or even offering a flower. The term "in their distress" (NIV) or "in their affliction" (RSV) implies their time of need, not only to visit those in prosperity, as the Pharisees did, along with their long prayers.

The Church sins by being absent in the involvement with the poor, the downtrodden, and the sick. Only very recently that some churches are breaking new ground and starting to see the great needs that the AIDS pandemic is bringing to the world. The church is slowly moving from the judgmental attitude against the AIDS pandemic and launching herself into a more intentional ministry to those who are affected by such a disease. Saddleback Church in California, through the efforts of its founding pastor, has initiated a new effort to reach out to those with AIDS. The initiative was named "Disturbing Voices," and drew about 2,000 pastors in a meeting held in December 2005. Alan Witchey, executive director of AIDS Services Foundation in Orange County, had this to say about the help they received from Saddleback Church, "A group like Saddleback is late to the table in terms of stepping up to help, but they're stepping up to help at a wonderful level." Later on he added, "We try to practice the same kind of thing that we want from people. We don't morally judge who's supporting us. We wouldn't turn our back." While many are looking for the pandemic in Africa and other poor areas of the world, it is about time for the Church to step up to the task of ministering to those who are dieing of AIDS in these United States as well. While many are looking for the

Tsunamis around the world, it is now time for the Church to take up the task of ministering to those who are affected by mega disasters in these United States too. It took a major disaster in New Orleans and surroundings to wake up the Church for such a great need. Katrina became a symbol of unity for the Church in many fronts: whereas the Government was so late in providing a substantial response, the Church was quicker to respond; she was there and continues to be there. Three years have past from that natural disaster at the time of this writing and even to this day we see the presence of the Church in the Louisiana and Mississippi areas. More of this should be seen as we continue to see that the love of God is in our hearts, moving us to help our neighbors here and abroad.

The Church has a lot to learn from the story of the Good Samaritan; maybe this is the time for all of us to humbly come to the feet of the Master and learn again what does it mean to serve those who at first sight are not even our friends. The True Religion, as we will continue to learn in this Epistle is Love in Action.

It Is Sanctified by God

The text continues to offer more light towards our understanding of the True Religion. It reads, "and to keep oneself from being polluted by the world." This is a key issue in differentiating the True Religion from any other. Not only the True Religion is directed to God only, not only does it point to our relationship with our neighbor, it is sanctified by God. This is important to realize because there are many attempts of self-sanctification in various religions. There are people in other religions who are called "holy" and there is reason for that. But the teaching of James does not bring to us any attempt to modify the centrality of the Holiness of God in our lives.

This idea of sanctification leads us to Paul's teaching in Romans. The Apostle to the Gentiles reminds us that our Christian life is not a reservoir of theological axioms; rather, all that has been taught to us as sound doctrine must be demonstrated in a practical way as well. It is the same principle of James and his wisdom. The parallel of this text and that of Romans 12:1-2 is somewhat remarkable. Paul urges his audience to offer a reasonable, or spiritual worship to God, by offering themselves as a living sacrifice to the Lord. This is the essence of worship, this is the center of James teaching about the pure and faultless religion. Then, Paul expands that concept into a similar idea of sanctification: By not walking according to patterns that the world. J. B. Phillips translated that verse in a very compelling way, "Don't let the world around you squeeze you into its own mold, but let God remold your minds from within, so that you may prove in practice that the plan of God is good, meets all the demands and moves toward the goal of true maturity" (Romans 12:2). This is an excellent parallel for what James writes, commanding us "to keep oneself from being polluted by the world."

The normal approaches to the pollution of our souls bring some old fashioned excuses, such as: "Everybody is doing it, so that's okay to do it," "It is cool!" Others venture to say, "I will just try this once..." And yet, some others go more "scientific" in their approach, "People are the product of their own environment..." The truth is that friendship with the world is enmity with God. This is the same as to "be molded by the world." James will talk about this very issue in Chapter 4 of his Epistle. Suffice is to say that one will keep his or her life undefiled by not allowing the world to mold his or her life.

A holy life is an imperative from God because it is his will that we be holy: "You shall be holy, for I am holy" (1 Peter 1:16). This is the evidence of the work of *Sanctification* in the life of the believer. "It is God's will that you should be sanctified," wrote Paul to the Thessalonians (1 Thessalonians 4:3). Sanctification is the work of the Holy Spirit in our lives but it will be manifested only when the believer shows evidence of his or her true religion; that is, the working of God in the Christian life from beginning to the end.

True Religion is our way of worship to God through our love to our neighbor and as we keep ourselves away from the influences of the world. In a nutshell, it is better summarized in the Law of Jesus Christ as found in Matthew 22:37-40, "Jesus said to him, 'You shall love the LORD your God with all your heart, with all your soul, and with all your mind.' This is the first and great commandment. And the second is like it: 'You shall love your neighbor as yourself.' On these two commandments hang all the Law and the Prophets." (NKJV).

The Wisdom Of James

As we continue to adore our Lord God Almighty and his Son, our Lord Jesus Christ, under the powerful ministry of the Holy Spirit, let us worship him, the Only God, Eternal and Majestic, with all our lives. As we do so, let us show to the world that we are his children indeed. By faith and by deed.

Chapter 3

The Testing of Our Faith

James 1:2-4

George Muller once said, "God delights to increase the faith of his children. We ought, instead of wanting no trials before victory, no exercise for patience, to be willing to take them from God's hands as a means. Trials, obstacles, difficulties, and sometimes defeats, are the very food of faith."

James had authority in calling his brothers and sisters to rejoice in the time of trials; as the leader in the Church of Jerusalem, he had witnessed the killing of Stephen, the decapitation of James, brother of John, the persecution of the Church and its consequences: widows, orphans, people scattered all over because of the fierce attacks from the Jews. The list is long. He was not an academician who did some word study on the issue of trials; he was one of those who were suffering them first hand. Therefore, he calls them "brethren," that is to say, "Not only do I sympathize with you, I am included in this time of trials and tribulations."

This chapter has great and transforming insights for us. It will show that suffering is a glorious opportunity for the growth of our faith. I remember meeting with Brother Andrew when I was a seminarian in Brazil back in 1979. Talking about the persecuted Church, he told me that we [Brazilians] would surely get to know who were the true believers if the church in Brazil went through a hard time of persecution. Of course he was talking about the Communist persecution going on behind the Iron Curtain, mostly in the former Soviet Union at that time. But I remember when I was working in the inland towns and villages of Paraíba and Pernambuco states, in Northeast Brazil: I often heard about persecution against the *crentes*, the believers, by the Roman Catholics, mostly by their clergy. I remember also witnessing the joy that our brothers and sisters had on their faces and, mostly, in their hearts for the privilege of being scorned and ridiculed because of their faith. The first part of this passage will help us better understand the virtues of a life under trial. As our faith is tested, let us count it as a motive of joy, not of sadness. Thus, as we move on, let us approach the trials of our faith as a motive of spiritual joy. It points to the joy of being tested in our faith.

Another aspect of this passage relates to the virtue of patience. George MacDonald once said, "The principal part of faith is patience." If on the one hand, we experience the joy of being tested in our faith through trials and tribulations, on the other hand we will experience the grace of God in giving us patience to go through the test. The text points to the fact that "the testing of our faith develops perseverance." We may not see how it happens during the hard times in our lives, but we eventually will realize later that those were the key moments in our spiritual journey.

I might add at this point that the testing of our faith will lead us to the wisdom we need for our walk with God during our pilgrimage on earth, in a short sentence: the wisdom to persevere. It is the refinement of our faith at its best; it is when, as Peter teaches us in his first letter, the time we go through the crucible of purification of our faith, turning it into something more precious than gold or silver. In this case, we will explore also the benefits of going through the hardships of our faith journey. This important test of our faith is necessary and we will rejoice with its outcome.

We Face Trials and Tribulations

The text points to the opportunity of growth in our lives as the time when we face "trials of many kinds." In order to better understand this concept, we should discuss the meaning of those

The Wisdom Of James

terms. We should firstly consider what "Trials" is not: The Greek word *peirasmos* has two distinct translations, and the context will determine that the meaning here is different from the one found in 1:13-14. This particular text suggests that "Trials" means "external adversities" such as affliction, persecution, and trial of any kind. The other term means "inner impulse to [do] evil." We will discuss the latter in the future, which will then open our understanding for the meaning of temptations, instead of trials or tribulations.

There is also a difference also between *joy* and *happiness*. It seems difficult for us to make sense of this verse, because we are so used to equal a good life as totally void of difficulties. We have the tendency of comparing joyfulness with happiness; the former is an inner strength that supercedes the momentum; it perpetuates the constancy of a state of mind, heart and soul. The latter is more related to the immediate feelings or reactions that we have under certain circumstances; happiness deals more with immediate feelings, the state of what is happening now. We may call it *hedonism*; in our case, *Christian hedonism*, "the doctrine that pleasure is the chief good in life." The difference is remarkable, but we tend to lean more towards the attitude of happiness: if we are not having pleasure; that is, having fun, we do not have joy. There is an Arab proverb that says, "Sunshine alone creates deserts." We must understand that our Christian life is full of trials and tribulations.

The lack of understanding in this area—that is, between these two terms—has brought a great deal of misconceptions about the Christian Faith. This seems to be the case for the growth of a number of churches that preach a theology that emphasizes only the "happiness" part of life. By that, I want to touch base with the so-called "theology of prosperity." I am not against the term prosperity at all. I truly believe that the Bible has a lot to teach us about the prosperity of the righteous (but also the lack of that prosperity). Abraham is a classic example of prosperity in the Bible: a man who left his home, his family, everything to obey a call that he had from God. The Scripture shows that he prospered abundantly. The book of Job, another classic example, shows a man who lost everything—family, possessions, his own health—and later, when his time of trial was over, God prospered him more than before. The examples are many but this is not the time for a more elaborated exposition of this doctrine. The problem, however, is that contemporary teachings in this area have misled thousands of well intentioned people and given them a faulty understanding of their faith. It is exactly here that we must learn how to differentiate between joy and happiness so we may take a different stand on the issue of trials and temptations.

Jesus Christ never promised an easy life for his disciples. The well known cliché says, "Jesus never promised a rose garden." We share in his suffering "in order that we may also share in his glory" (Romans 8:17). Also, he told his disciples, "I have told you these things, so that in me you may have peace. In this world you will have trouble. But take heart! I have overcome the world" (John 16:33).

Spiritual Joy

The Christian Faith is filled with paradoxes. In fact, there is a wonderful book about the teachings of Jesus Christ that has a very interesting title, *The Upside-Down Kingdom*. It reflects well what I want to convey in this line of thought: Our faith is paradoxical because it has the impact of a message that does not seem to fit the proclamations of the world. James writes, "consider it pure joy, my brothers, whenever you face trials of many kinds." This is a paradox!

There is a place for joy in the midst of suffering through many trials that we face daily. James is in harmony with the teaching of Peter, who also wrote about the trials of our faith. Peter admonished the Church in the Diaspora in the same way, "In this you greatly rejoice, though now for a little while you may have had to suffer grief in all kinds of trials" (1 Peter 1:6). Even so, the Lord will not allow us to suffer any temptation that will destroy our faith; on the contrary, he promises to be there for us. "No temptation has over-taken you except such as is common to man; but God is faithful, who will not allow you to be tempted beyond what you are able, but with the temptation will also make the way of escape, that you may be able to bear it" (1 Corinthians 10:13, NKJV).

The Apostles had joy when they suffered persecution, "The apostles left the Sanhedrin, rejoicing because they had been counted worthy of suffering disgrace for the Name" (Acts 5:41). Paul and Silas were singing praises to the Lord when in prison (Acts 16). Paul, once more, writes to the Romans saying that "we also rejoice in our sufferings, because we know that suffering produces perseverance" (Romans 5:3) and to the Philippians, while he was in prison, he commanded the followers of Jesus to "rejoice in the Lord always" (Philippians 4:4). But it is Jesus Christ who said it more clearer when he addressed the crowd in his sermon on the mount, "Blessed are you when people insult you, persecute you and falsely say all kinds of evil against you because of me. Rejoice and be glad, because great is your reward in heaven, for in the same way they persecuted the prophets who were before you" (Matthew 5:11-12).

If our lives are not under a certain amount of suffering; that is, facing trials, I think we are not being tested. Consider, as James suggests, a motive of joy, the many instances in our lives when things seem to not be working the way we want. We often do not understand what is going on until we realize that the Lord is sovereign and loving towards us. Kistemaker adds an important word when he comments on this passage, "The Christian ought to see the hand of God in all of life." In his commentary, he quotes William Cowper, who wrote the following verses,

God moves in a mysterious way
His wonders to perform;
He plants his footsteps in the sea,
And rides upon the storm.

Deep in unfathomable mines
of never failing skill,
He treasures up his bright designs
and works his sovereign will.

This text continues to illuminate our minds and to warm our hearts with a growing sense of God's presence in our lives. Even when we are facing difficult times, he is there for us. James knows that one would go through trials and tribulations, but the need for encouragement continues to be great. Not only are we called to consider it pure joy, we are also encouraged to persevere in our faith. We need to realize that patience is a key factor in the growth process of our faith.

The Importance of Trials in Our Life

We need to realize that trials and tribulations in our lives have a divine purpose. The Lord wants to have mature children; therefore, trials are part of that process. We learn from Paul that we continue to work out our salvation under God's sovereign care; but we have the responsibility to respond to God's prompting in our lives. It is a process; salvation is given once for all, but it takes time for us to endure the journey from the cross to the gates of Heaven. This journey has a final destination. Paul puts it this way, "Not that I have already obtained this, or have already been made perfect, but I press on to take hold of that for which Christ Jesus took hold of me" (Philippians 3:12).

Because our faith is not passive, it is perfected in an active way. The Epistle of James is clear in leading us to the understanding that our faith will be known only as we demonstrate it in a visible and tangible way. Again, it is James who teaches us that faith without action is dead (James 2:17). Here we see the importance of trials and tribulations in our lives. They come sometimes in a most unexpected way; someone in our family suddenly is involved in a car accident, another dear friend is diagnosed with cancer, a spouse file for divorce, a son or a daughter faces the pain of an unexpected layoff. The list can become really big, but real. There is nothing you and I can do at the moment; but the trial is there, in front of us. We may get mad at God, disappointed about the new circumstance that surrounds us. This is the turning point in our growing up curve; it is through this process that we get closer to God. But we must respond to whatever comes upon us with faith and a sacred determination that we will overcome those obstacles entirely with the help of the Father. It is then that our faith starts to show evidence of growth; it becomes more and more strengthened, purified, golden.

Developing Our Patience

Deep inside we know that the testing of our faith develops patience. I should at this time explore the meaning of this important word in its original context. The term *hupomone* can be translated in different ways. It can be translated as *perseverance*, the ability to keep in focus, looking ahead despite of many obstacles; it can also be rendered as *steadfastness*, to be firm, not changing, to be settled; *quietness*, to have inner peace; *patience*, to wait with a sense of peace, to be focused on the final result; and, as put by a commentator, "steadfast endurance and triumphant trust."

We face circumstances in our lives that often push us to the limit; time is a precious commodity and as such, it dictates the immediateness of things as the most acceptable value for success. We live in a time when we have lost the meaning of patience, or perseverance, or steadfastness. We want everything instantly: instant coffee, instant teller machines, instant marriages, instant food, and the list is ever growing. The bottom line is that we have lost the meaning of waiting; therefore, it is very hard for us to apply this concept in our daily life. It seems hard for most of us when the idea of waiting for God's direction, waiting for God's move. We have, nonetheless, illustrations from a number of people who have succeeded in their lives, attained the goals they had set, because they patiently kept their focus on what they aimed for. We see them as heroes, as role models, as inspirational characters for ourselves, our children, our students, and so forth. But James is here pointing to the fact that we do not need to be super heroes to attain the purposed goals that God has for us. Rather, he teaches that, through the hardships we face, we will develop a sense of focus, perseverance, and by faith we will get there.

There are some biblical passages about this virtue that I think to be appropriate at this point. Starting with James, we read about the example of Job, "As you know, we consider blessed those who have persevered. You have heard of Job's perseverance and have seen what the Lord finally brought about. The Lord is full of compassion and mercy" (5:11). Solomon's wisdom shows that "A man's wisdom gives him patience" (Proverbs 19:11a). The Author of

Hebrews commends those who persevered by faith, "These were all commended for their faith, yet none of them received what had been promised" (Hebrews 11:39). Paul speaks elsewhere about our role in the sharing of our Christian life with patience, "The Lord teach you and enable you to love as God loves and to be patient as Christ is patient."

Perseverance Works Out Maturity

The text reads that, "Perseverance must finish its work so that you may be mature and complete." This is the goal, the purpose of God for all of us. It is his purpose that we may become perfect; that is, complete. That purpose is linked with a very powerful word *teleios* (from the Greek), meaning "to reach an end." The Lord wants us to have accomplished lives.

This is God's purpose from beginning to end: that we be like his Son Jesus Christ, that in him we will be found mature, complete, whole, full of integrity of life. This is what Paul teaches us, "We proclaim him, admonishing and teaching everyone with all wisdom, so that we may present everyone perfect in Christ." This spiritual maturity is attained through the perseverance of the believer. Paul, once more, writes that "endurance produces character" (Romans 5:4). And Peter, "For this very reason, make every effort to add to your faith goodness; and to goodness, knowledge; and to knowledge, self-control; and to self-control, perseverance; and to perseverance, godliness; and to godliness, love" (2 Peter 1:5-7). This is what we understand for "not lacking anything." It shows that the mature Christian has everything. "The Lord is my Shepherd, therefore I lack nothing" (Psalm 23:1).

God will not allow us to be under trials, tribulations, and temptations that we cannot stand (1 Corinthians 10:13). He is fair and faithful; he wants the best for us. Maybe we do not understand why hardships come to us; but one thing is for sure: the Lord is sovereign and in total control of our lives because he loves us. He is "full of compassion and mercy" (James 5:11). We will come back to more teaching on patience in the future; but now it is enough for us to understand that when our faith is tested, the testing of our faith will produce patience, perseverance, and steadfastness.

Kistemaker points out that, "God stands behind every trial and test. He wants us to know this by experience, so that we not only see his hand but also feel it." We also read in the Heidelberg Catechism that, "All things, in fact, come to us not by chance, but from his fatherly hand." It is key for us to understand these truths because they are the motivation for our joy and perseverance under trials. Only those who do not know this important truth will succumb, failing the test of their faith. This is why we must go to the Word of God in order to learn the depths of God's purpose for our lives. I would like to leave with you a verse from the Book of Psalms as a wonderful reminder of his love for us: "The LORD will fulfill his purpose for me; your love, O LORD, endures forever — do not abandon the works of your hands" (Psalm 138:8).

Chapter 4

Asking for Wisdom

James 1:5-8

We come a step further in our understanding of trials and tribulations. At this point, however, it is the first opportunity that James has to introduce the theme of prayer. James helps us a lot in learning about "asking God"; that is, praying to God. Here is the entry point to this important theological fact: *we must go to the Lord in prayer; our help sure comes from him and not from other people.*

We also learn from James that, instead of asking God to remove the trial, we should go to the Lord in prayer and ask for wisdom in order to go through that difficult time in our lives. We are encouraged to seek him as the source of our strength in times of wilderness. I am always reminded that our walk with the Lord is sometimes filled with ups and downs; it is not unusual to find out that we may be either on the top of a mountain or in a deep valley. It is very difficult to even realize that we are walking in the midst of a dry season in our lives; but those days are precious for us. Nonetheless, it is then that we really need to come to the Lord and ask for wisdom to continue yet another day.

Another aspect of this important truth is that James equals wisdom with True Religion; that is, we will go through life only if we learn from God what is his will for us. True Religion is the wisdom that we receive from the Lord which will reconnect us to

The Wisdom Of James

him as we worship him in spirit and in truth (cf. John 4:24). Adam Clarke suggests that this kind of wisdom is "the thorough practical knowledge of God, of one's self, and of a Saviour."

This chapter will help us better understand how to handle the trials and tribulations that we face in our walk as Christians. We have already learned that we should rejoice when our faith is tested, and that we should realize that the testing of our faith is God's way to strengthen our walk with him. Now we will learn how to go through this process of growth. I'd like to call this growth process the "Wisdom for the Journey." As fellow sojourners, we need that kind of wisdom; we cannot afford to walk through our pilgrimage alone. The wisdom that we ask God will enable us to go through our journey together as we worship the Lord.

Realizing That We Need Wisdom

It is the perception of this passage that leads us to realize that we lack wisdom sometimes and that we need to come to the Lord in prayer and supplication, asking him for that amount of wisdom we so desperately need. We read, "If any of you lacks wisdom." Here James plays with two ideas in this paragraph, we call it a "Hebrew parallelism." He says in verse 4 that perseverance (or patience) makes us complete, "lacking in nothing." But at the same time he starts verse 5 suggesting that "if any of you lacks wisdom." This is not a contradiction, but a paradox. We may be found lacking until the perfect is molded in us; until we attain the stature of Jesus Christ, we will be lacking something. The goal, that is, the *teleios* of God for our lives is the perfection of the image of his Son in us (cf. Romans 8:29; Philippians 3:12-14), but we will get there only through the process of sanctification and spiritual maturity. Therefore, we must realize that we lack something; James goes direct to the point by suggesting that all we need is wisdom.

This is a most humbling situation for us, but a necessary one. The best way to receive God's help is to realize that we need his help in the first place. As an example, it is impossible to help a person with alcohol problems unless that person first realizes that she is sick, that he is dependent, addicted to alcohol. The same occurs to us in this

The Wisdom Of James

situation: unless we realize that we lack wisdom, we will not ask for God's help in this important area of our lives.

Again, comparing verses 4 and 5, we come to the realization that wisdom comes from the Lord, not from ourselves. For this reason, we must ask God for it. John A. Bengel puts it this way: "Patience is more in the power of a good man than wisdom; the former is to be exercised, the latter is to be asked for." Unless we realize that we need God's wisdom for the journey, we will walk like a blind person in the deepest of darkness without a single light post to point us to the direction we are going.

In a time of so much confusion, we need wisdom. We live in an epoch of unwise days; the growing lack of nurture for our families, the misconceptions about life, the misappropriation of what is right and what is wrong are just symptoms of our age. Unfortunately we see this same pattern in our churches; people with divided allegiances, brothers and sisters with lack of a solid commitment to the Wisdom of God. Although James will talk about wisdom with some more details later, he is introducing this important area of True Religion at this moment.

Learning More About Wisdom

The word "wisdom" is used in three verses in James; all of them related to the same thing. We will learn more about it in the future (James 3), but for now it is sufficient to have just a glance of the concept and then try to understand better the need for it.

But before we move on, we should stop and address another key element in our inquiry about wisdom. There is a difference between *wisdom* and *knowledge*. Knowledge without wisdom is foolishness. Someone may have a great baggage of knowledge and be a complete fool. Take the story of the Young Ruler who came to visit Jesus Christ as an example. He knew the Law of Moses well but lacked in the understanding of its deepest meaning. The Lord confronted him with the very Truth that he had knowledge about, but the commitment to the wisdom of the Truth was more than he could handle. When told by Jesus that he should change his allegiance from his wealth to him, the young man failed terribly. Luke

51

reports that, "when he heard these things, he became very sad, for he was extremely rich" (Luke 18:23). The opposite takes place with the other man who understood the meaning of the Kingdom of God and did everything he could to get it. This is well explained by the Lord in two small parables: The Parables of the Hidden Treasure and of the Pearl of Great Value (Matthew 13:44-45). On a different approach, another example of foolishness is told by Jesus in the Parable of the Rich Fool, who wanted to accumulate his wealth and have fun for the rest of his life, only without knowing that he was set to die that very day (Luke 12:13-21). If we consider knowledge as synonymous to wisdom, Paul is right in his concern about his own people when he writes to the Romans, "I bear them witness that they have a zeal for God, but not according to knowledge. For, being ignorant of the righteousness that comes from God, and seeking to establish their own, they did not submit to God's righteousness" (Romans 10:2-3). I believe that wisdom and knowledge must go together; one depends on each other.

But before I bring a tentative definition of wisdom, I want to share what Adam Clarke describes about knowledge. He distinguishes knowledge in four areas: "*Intelligence*, the object of which is intuitive truths; *Wisdom*, which is employed in finding out the best end; *Prudence*, which regulates the whole conduct through life; and *Art*, which provides infallible rules to reason by." There is great value in knowledge; I am not suggesting that it contradicts wisdom. In fact, the Church nowadays has been filled with the lack of knowledge; many a wise person have stood before the congregation without any knowledge of the Scriptures, for example. According to Clarke, then, wisdom is included in the corpus of knowledge that someone has acquired. Wisdom, therefore, "is a good judgment in the face of the demands made by humans and specifically by the Christian experience. It is a practical exercise of the knowledge that the Lord is giving to us. In a more practical way, wisdom is the discernment of God's will for our lives; it is the understanding that God's purpose for us is the best way to go." As an illustration, I think Paul is accurate in defining "wisdom" by showing us that it depends on our unswerving surrender to God's will. After urging his audience to present themselves as a living sacrifice to God that is "holy and acceptable to God, which is your spiritual worship," he calls them to a true conversion and real transformation in their lives. All of that has a purpose, "that by testing you may discern what is the will of God, what is good and acceptable and perfect" (Romans 12:1-2).

Asking for Wisdom with the Right Attitude

James often deals with the issue of attitude; not the one we sometimes try to impose to others, but an attitude that is clearly acceptable to God. This is True Religion. He deals with this issue here, and the attitude he is talking about is the one of faith; we should ask in faith. This is what makes the difference; it is far from being a mantra or even a mechanical repetition of mere words. When we come to the Lord in prayer we must approach his throne of grace with the faith that he has bestowed upon us.

Of course, this attitude before God involves our worship to him as a whole; not only as a time of singing praises. Our posture before the Lord — our *cultus* — is shown from inside, it comes from our innermost being. Peter H. Davids makes an effort to translate what "religion" is as an attempt to give us the idea of how we come before the Lord. In his words, "the specific practices James has in mind are unclear, but would include the religious activities of prayer, fasting, and worship of his community (and perhaps the keeping of the ritual law as well, assuming it was a Jewish Christian community)." But here, I would like to attain to the fact that our primary attitude before the Lord is that of complete submission to his will. As we come to him in prayer, which is part of our *cultus*, we must bow down before his sovereignty and realize that all graces come from him and from him alone. Prayer is, therefore, one of the chief parts of the True Religion.

A Generous Gift

Wisdom is a generous gift from God. The Lord gives it graciously and without any reservation. He is delighted to give wisdom to those who want to follow him. He gives rain to good and bad people (common grace). He is open to hear our prayers without any reservation; sometimes we are afraid he will not listen to our petitions. But he is generous and all giving; awaiting for our prayers and asking. Kistemaker puts it this way, "God gives generously without reservation; therefore, he expects the believer to come to him in prayer without reservation."

There is great comfort in knowing this truth. Jesus Christ brings forth a wonderful teaching on the issue of asking; sometimes we do not grasp its entire meaning because we feel undeserving. In one sense, we actually do not deserve anything—if we look from a negative angle—because our sin has made us enemies of God. This is why we so desperately need his grace, without which we will never come to him in the first place. But here, the teaching goes beyond the undeserving as related to our salvation. It has to do with those who have been graciously saved and now are free to enjoy the blessings of being children of God. In that case, we certainly are deserving, not in a meritorious way, of course, but because of Jesus' sacrifice and gracious redemption, we are invited by God to come to him and ask for whatever we are in need. The teaching in this area is vast and I would like to be as concise as I can at this point. The Good Savior once spoke that we should "ask, and it will be given to you; seek, and you will find; knock, and it will be opened to you" (Matthew 7:7). The amazing thing in his teaching is what comes next. He suggests that like a father, his Father would give abundantly what we are in need for—in this particular case, the Lord was talking about the Holy Spirit (Matthew 7:7-11; cf. Luke 11:9-13). In his teaching we see that a father—my father, for example—would never give me a scorpion or a serpent if I had first asked for a loaf of bread or a fish. The same is true with our Father in Heaven; he will give us what is good for us. Wisdom is a good thing to ask for.

The other aspect of God's generosity is that he gives it abundantly. The Lord Almighty has generous hands and gives away gifts that we cannot even imagine before. Paul has a wonderful way of putting it when he wrote to the Ephesians. After he writes about his prayer for spiritual strength for the Church, he ends that paragraph with a hymn of praise, "Now to him who is able to do far more abundantly than all that we ask or think, according to the power at work within us, to him be glory in the church and in Christ Jesus throughout all generations, forever and ever. Amen" (Ephesians 3:20-21). This describes the generosity of God in granting us his wisdom.

Asking With Faith

Here we find the only condition we must follow. It is entirely by faith. This attitude is of key importance in our walk with God; much more in our time of need. We must come to him entirely in faith. As and example, in Jeremiah's mind, he grasped the word of God in a very special way. For God, to have faith requires an unconditional surrender of our hearts; we must put our hearts completely in his hands and expect that he will certainly listen to our prayer. This is how Jeremiah wrote the oracle of the Lord, "Then you will call upon me and come and pray to me, and I will hear you. You will seek me and find me. When you seek me with all your heart" (Jeremiah 29:12-13). As we can see, it requires all of ourselves. It is when we abandon ourselves entirely in God's hands that he will answer our prayers.

Jesus has another interesting way of putting it when he talks about answered prayers. For him, there is not even a problem with the tense of the verbs that he uses. Matthew recorded it in a future tense, which in itself binds God's word to what will happen: "And whatever you ask in prayer, you will receive, if you have faith" (Matthew 21:22). But Mark did record Jesus words with a very different verb tense. In Mark's understanding of Jesus' teaching, he heard the Lord say that the answer of our prayers are so certain that we should consider it done. This is how he put it in his Gospel, "Therefore I tell you, whatever you ask in prayer, believe that you have received it, and it will be yours" (Mark 11:24).

This is what I believe to be the right attitude in our asking. We must come to the Lord in total surrender, in total commitment to him, in total and unconditional faith. This leads us to the next step in James' teaching.

The Split-Mind Syndrome

Those who lack faith have a split-minded attitude towards God. The Greek word, *dipsichos*, suggests a person with "two souls." In a nutshell, this is a sin, the sin of doubting. In Romans we learn that a person who is not sure of what is to be done, commits sin; better explained, Paul was talking about passing judgment on others in what they should eat or not. In that case, if the person was not sure and ate in doubt was sinning. He ends his line of though with the following statement, "For whatever does not proceed from faith is sin" (Romans 14:23b). The same occurs when the person does not ask God with faith. That person has a double-minded attitude. James compares that person to the wave of the sea, which "is driven and tossed by the wind." This is a rather negative way of putting the issue, but it cannot be well understood otherwise. James is not shy about saying negative things to his readers. He writes as a prophet and knows that the truth, like a coin, has two sides. In order to understand one, we should know what the other looks like. He is not dualist in his statements, however; he is objective in what he wants to convey. The bottom line is simple: someone who does not have faith, is a doubtful person, a person with a split-minded relationship with God.

We are called to trust in the Lord with all our hearts, completely. If we do not trust him, our faith is not there. Here we see the link between wisdom and faith, they go together. The wise person is complete in faith; that is, it is through the lenses of faith that one will receive the wisdom that God gives. We must trust the Lord completely and unconditionally. This is in perfect harmony with the teaching of the Author of Hebrews who says that, "without faith it is impossible to please him, for whoever would draw near to God must believe that he exists and that he rewards those who seek him" (Hebrews 11:6). Faith has everything to do with complete trust; unless we put our faith in God, we cannot please him.

Another way to understand the efficacy of our faith is presented by the Psalmist. We learn from him that we should trust the Lord with our hearts. One of my favored passages in Scripture brings this truth with power, "Commit your way to the LORD; trust in him, and he will act. He will bring forth your righteousness as the light, and your justice as the noonday. Be still before the LORD and wait patiently for him..." (Psalm 37:5-7a). One particular thing in this statement gives me the perspective on God's action: He will act only if we act. It seems paradoxical, but it is very logical. If we "believed" after he acted, our act of believing would be completely void, a total nonsense. Faith moves the hands of God into action. If we ask him in faith, he will certainly act.

Our Lord Jesus Christ also was very direct in pointing out that faith has a powerful effect in God's presence. He said many strong words about faith—sometimes calling his disciples of men without faith— and challenging them, and us today, to launch ourselves completely into our Father's arms. Faith has a tremendous power; if we only knew it, we would transform our world. But one of the words of Jesus that has an impact on this particular thought is found in Matthews. The Lord discusses the issue of faith as compared with doubt, as we can verify, "And Jesus answered them, 'Truly, I say to you, *if you have faith and do not doubt*, you will not only do what has been done to the fig tree, but even if you say to this mountain, "Be taken up and thrown into the sea," it will happen. And whatever you ask in prayer, you will receive, if you have faith'" (Matthew 21:21-22, *emphasis added*).

Matthew Henry says, "Let us confess our want of wisdom to God and daily ask it of him." Wisdom will enable us to visualize our Christian life the way God has designed it to be. It will help us face the trials and tribulations with "pure joy," but also will help us understand the perfect will of God for our lives.

Sometimes we are just like the father of the boy with an evil spirit, "Immediately the father of the child cried out and said, 'I believe; help my unbelief!'" (Mark 9:24). But let us also remember that Jesus Christ had had a wonderful word of hope for that man, "And Jesus said to him, 'If you can! All things are possible for one who believes'" (Mark 9:23). That was the great comfort for a man who lacked something, but Jesus was there for him.

We are dealing with a very small part of the teaching on wisdom at this point. The major emphasis from James is on our realization that we may be lacking in it. But also, he is calling us to act upon

The Wisdom Of James

that need. In doing so, he is encouraging us to seek the Lord with all our hearts, in complete faith. The Lord is generous in giving to "all without reproach." Therefore, it is up to us to come to him and ask. With that in mind, I want to remind ourselves that God will act only after we act; this is the mystery of faith.

Chapter 5

Trials and Temptations

James 1:2-18

Ernest Trice Thompson once wrote, "Temptation is a part of life. No one is immune—at any age. For temptation is present wherever there is a choice to be made, not only between good and evil, but also between a higher and lower good. For some, it may be a temptation to sensual gratification; for others a temptation to misuse their gifts, to seek personal success at the cost of the general welfare, to seek a worthy aim by unworthy means, to lower their ideal to win favor with the electorate, or with their companions and associates." I want to introduce a necessary parenthesis in this book to provide some fundamental explanation about the terminology used by James for temptation as compared to trials. As we are going to see below, the word is the same in the Greek text, but the meaning of it will be made clear only through the context of what James is trying to pass on to us. For that matter, I need to take the longer text in chapter 1 of the Epistle as the basis for this parenthetical chapter.

This longer passage brings together the two aspects of the word *peirasmos*, which could be translated as *trial* or *temptation*. As we learned before, this word must be understood in its own context. In the context of James 1:2 and 12, the same word "trial" has basically two different meanings. In the former, *trial* is an exterior imposition; that is, tribulations that come from outside. In the latter, *trial* has an added meaning that includes the possibility of an inner struggle with the presence of tribulation. Thus, James is aware that the many trials that we are under can become potential doors for fierce temptations against us. His goal in this longer passage is to help us to realize that danger and stand firm in our faith against the many temptations that may come during times of trial.

The text also offers a few key verbs that will help us overcome trials and temptations; thus securing a blessed life with God:

1. *Understand* the value of our faith
2. *Ask* God for his wisdom
3. *Take pride* in our high position in the Kingdom of God
4. *Expect* God's promises of blessings to come
5. *Distinguish* between trials and temptations
6. *Realize* how God is good and perfect
7. *Remember* how we received our birth from God.

The core of this chapter is to deal with the differentiation between *Trials* and *Temptations*. We have already learned about the former at considerable length; therefore, I will spend time dealing with the latter now. It is necessary that we learn where one ends and the other begins; there is the danger of us falling into a gray area when we go through different trials. It is imperative to know how to differentiate them. In our daily struggle, we find ourselves bombarded by all kinds of attacks and snares. Some are created by ourselves, they are the traps that our flesh puts before us; others are created by the enemy who is working without stop to crush us and destroy the seed of faith that the Lord has planted in our hearts. Yet another source of temptations is the world which does not cease to threaten our faith with numerous propositions. Each new day, we have new facets of the world's temptations flashing right in front of our very eyes. Here is the reason why we must be well versed in the teachings of the Scripture in order to know how to see which is which; at the same time that we are expected to rejoice when we go through trials and tribulations, we are also expected to know when the many temptations are trying to destroy our daily walk with the Lord.

Watch Out! Not Everyone Will Endure the Test

Since Adam and Eve, humans have been put to the test. In our Christian walk, as we have been learning, we have been under a life process that seems to be very hard to go through sometimes. We need to be aware that our trials will be so hard that they could turn into temptations. The main trigger of the Fall was not the trial, or testing in itself, but the temptation that Eve and Adam fell into. They failed because they did not realize that they were being tested; therefore, beginning with Eve, they gave room to their own desire to become like God. As soon as they fell they realized that they had sinned against God and tried to flee from him. In similar ways, we fail in our trials only to remember later, in most cases much later than we expected, that we were able to avoid them should we had known the difference between trials and temptations.

What James is trying to pass on to his readers and to all of us now is that not everyone will endure the trials in their Christian pilgrimage, unless we realize the danger of being tempted. The Bible is clear when it says that we all have corrupt hearts, "The heart is deceitful above all things, and desperately corrupt; who can understand it?" (Jeremiah 17:9, RSV). For that reason, we are called to watch out lest we fall in the various temptations that can come with the trials that we may be facing on a daily basis. C. S. Lewis puts it well in his book *The Screwtape Letters*, "No man knows how bad he is until he has tried to be good. There is a silly idea about that good people don't know what temptation means."

What humbles me the most is the realization that we all are prone to fail by falling into temptation. No one of us is exempt, all are just one step away of falling into any trap that is set before us. That is why we must be watchful, depending on God's grace for the entire journey. This reminds me of King David, who fell into temptation and because of that his sin was horrendous at the sight of God. In one of his many psalms, he wrote about the danger of falling into the snare that the enemy has prepared for him. He puts it this way, "For you are my rock and my fortress; and for your name's sake you lead me and guide me; you take me out of the net they have hidden for me, for you are my refuge" (Psalm 31:3-4). Several other versions use the term *trap*, instead of net. It is in times of trials, persecutions and tribulations that temptations become more real; therefore, we must trust the Lord for help and refuge then.

Learning the Difference

When the trials are getting harder and harder, we often feel that we are not able to handle them. This is when we are in danger of opening up ourselves to any kind of temptation. That is why James says, "If any of you lacks wisdom, he should ask God." Wisdom plays a very important role in the process of sanctification and will help us not to fall into temptation. It will enable us to realize that trials will lead us to a perfect life and that they work for our good, instead of our destruction. Conversely, lack of wisdom leads the Christian to live a miserable life, in which he or she is constantly failing because of temptation.

Trials happen in our lives to test our faith. They are outward circumstances that will produce endurance (patience, steadfastness) for a purpose: To make us into mature Christians. Temptations, on the other hand, are inward and deeply rooted in our hearts. They are also part of our test, but they are testing our moral strength to resist sin. In the context of James, the Church was going through a tremendous amount of trail. They had been dispersed around the known world of his day, mostly due to the fierce persecution that the Jewish leaders had imposed onto them. They had, in some form— maybe politically or sociologically—, lost their identity as Jewish citizens because they no longer were following the *status quo* of the nation of Israel. Their widows and orphans had lost the welfare of the state, which was basically exercised through the Temple in Jerusalem. Most of the Church members were destitute and in dire straits.

As the years went by and the Church spread among the Gentiles, the persecution was not different. The Christians became a threat to the non-Jewish *status quo* as well. As they were coming to the Lord Jesus Christ, their newfound faith and allegiance demanded a severance with the patterns of the world. They no longer put their money in businesses that were not in line with the Kingdom of God; for

The Wisdom Of James

example, the Church in Ephesus and Philippi became a threat for the businesses related to the idolatrous cults that generated great portion of the local economy in those cities. Thus, the Christian people were persecuted because of that. At a political level, the Christians pledged their allegiance to Jesus Christ, not to the Roman Emperor. They stopped saying "Ave Caesar!" to say "Ave Jesus!" Caesar was no longer their lord, but Jesus of Nazareth was now their Lord. Caesar was no longer their god, but Jesus of Nazareth, the Son of God. Rome was no longer their city of gold (neither Jerusalem, for that matter), but the New Jerusalem, the New Zion, the Eternal City of Gold (cf. Hebrews 12:22-23a; Revelation 21-22) had become the center of their hope. Thus, the Christian population was persecuted; many became martyrs, their blood became the seed of the growing Church around the world. Even so, many succumbed to the temptation of retracting from their faith; many preferred to return to their old allegiances in order not to die. But those who persevered to the very end, to the point of shedding their own blood for the sake of the Gospel, they received their crowns in Heaven (Revelation 2:10).

We learn the difference between trials and temptations only when we are faced with the trials first. The healthy church is not that one with a large variety of programs. It is not the one with the most fantastic preacher or Bible scholar. A healthy church is not the one with no sign of problems. Rather, the healthy church is the one that is tested with fire. I remember years ago when I had a personal interview with Brother Andrew. It was in Recife, Brazil. I was a seminarian then, and I interviewed him for our Seminary's newspaper. The year was 1979. Brother Andrew made a statement that still lingers in my mind and heart: "Ehud, you will know who is a true believer only when persecution comes to Brazil." He was talking about the spread of Communism around the world then. He was trying to explain to me that, in his experience behind the Iron Curtain, the church was healthy because of the persecution that was taking place there. Only the faithful were able to stand; there was no chance for the weak. The same happens in China today. The Underground Church is strong; the state-approved church in China is not that strong. You see that there is a great difference between the two churches in China.

Because of our natural inclination to commit sin, when we do not know how to differentiate between trials and temptations, we find ourselves in the midst of the worse part of the testing of our faith; in other words, to know the difference between the two will show that we are mature children of God.

Trials come in different sizes and shapes, not only through visible persecution. I had the privilege of working with two precious churches in the states of Paraíba and Pernambuco, in my homeland. They were located in a very poor area and most of their members were facing great financial hardship at the time, along with a prolonged period of drought. It was a delight for me to observe how their faith was vivid, alive. It was through those times of harsh trials that they had their wonderful experience of faith with our Lord and Savior. I could see the contrast between their faith and that of some well-off churches in the big cities of their states.

Just Say "NO!"

There are four steps in the process of temptation: desire, enticement, conception of sin, and death. As an example, let us take the life of Judas Iscariot, the one who betrayed Jesus Christ: *Desire.* He was open to "steal" money. The Evangelist and Apostle John described his character in a very direct way, "He [Judas Iscariot] said this, not because he cared about the poor, but because he was a thief, and having charge of the moneybag he used to help himself to what was put into it" (John 12:6). *Enticement.* The money was the enticement for Judas betrayal. Of course, he was part of the Zealot party and he thought that launching Jesus up in the open, he would certainly liberate the people of Israel. But, it was the amount of money offered that motivated him to commit the sin. *Conception of sin.* This is the natural outcome of the former step. The motivation was there; but along with it, the conception of sin, the actualization of the fact. Finally, the result was *death.* Judas committed suicide after he realized that Jesus was an innocent man. I would like to ask you to apply those steps in the known examples that you may find in the Bible. They are not that different from Judas. Start with Adam and Eve, go through the Holy Word and you will find a consistent relationship of those four steps in the lives of people whose sins are mentioned in the Scripture. (Another classic example is Samson's life and demise). Then, I would like to suggest that you apply them to your own life. It is humbling to see that they apply to us as well. Speaking from my personal experience in life, I found out that I am not exempt of this sad reality. Therefore, I am always reminded of God's grace and mercy upon my life.

In all circumstances of our lives we are exposed to potential death by falling into temptation: Here we find four examples from the Bible that will help us better understand how to deal with temptation: A bad example, King David. A model to follow, Joseph of Egypt. A classic example, Job. The Supreme Example to follow, Jesus Christ, our Lord, who was tempted in everything but did not commit one single sin.

Many of us are familiar with the motto of a major campaign against drugs and alcohol, "Just say 'No!'" The same we can apply to our situation as fellow pilgrims, prone to fall in temptation. We have been endowed with the spiritual power to say "No!" to temptations. James teaches us what to do—we will deal with this passage in the future—but I would like to introduce it here now, "Submit yourselves therefore to God. Resist the devil and he will flee from you" (James 4:7).

The Unchangeable Gift from God

We live in a culture that has mastered the science of blaming others for its actions. This sad reality is due to the fact that we have been taught how to escape from our own responsibility. I should say that psychoanalysis is one of the key contributors to this situation today, if not dealt with responsibly. This problem is a hard thing to deal in counseling, for example. Usually, when a person seeks counseling, she or he may come with the preconceived idea that whatever he or she has done will be transferred to some other entity outside the inner realm of their own responsibility. There will probably be someone, something, or some event to blame for in the end of the course of sessions. This might sound like a mere generalization of a bigger issue, but the norm seems to fit this sad situation in many cases. With the exception of a few Christian counselors, most of the general approach to this matter follows what I am stating above.

In the same fashion that Adam blamed Eve and Eve blamed the Serpent; we try to blame someone else for our actions. Here James, acting as a Christian counselor, goes directly to the point. I think what he had in mind was a little bit like this, *"Okay brothers and sisters: Do not come up with the idea that God made you do it; don't even think about accusing God as the one who tempted you. Take full responsibility for your actions!"* His argument was clear and to the point: "God cannot be tempted with evil, and he himself tempts no one."

Instead, we should look at God as the one who gives us *every good gift from above.* God is Good! "Every good gift and every perfect gift is from above, coming from the Father of lights with whom there is no variation or shadow due to change." Again, we must emphasize that God does not change to accommodate our sins, to allow us to fall for a new and different wave of temptations. His precious gift, unchangeable as it is, is wrapped in his Truth: "Of his own will he brought us forth by the word of truth, that we should be a kind of firstfruits of his creatures."

Simply put, we need to realize that we are weak and frail. We are sick in our hearts to the point of betraying ourselves without even noticing it (Jeremiah 17:9). Even when we realize that we cannot help ourselves, that we are responsible for our own actions, we are reminded that God has given us an unchangeable gift, the gift of wisdom to deal with our trials and temptations.

Take for example the incident of King David with Bathsheba (2 Samuel 11-12). David committed that horrendous sin without even noticing that he was falling into a huge trap that the enemy had set before him. It took Nathan to come to him and, through a parable, bring the king to the realization of his sin. Here we see the example of God's grace and mercy upon David. Nathan, whose name means "gift," was sent to confront him with his need for repentance; today, we have the Holy Spirit working in the same manner in our lives. Back to James, wisdom is pair with the notion of that same gift that God gives us unconditionally in order to bring us to the realization of our state before him.

John Bunyan, the great Puritan, wrote the following: "Temptation provokes me to look upward to God." When we are faced with temptations, this is the only way for us to go through the hardest trials that we may encounter in our journey. Let us keep looking upward to God and find in him the strength for our daily walk with the Lord.

As we consider the unchangeable gift from God, we turn again to James' affirming words, "He chose to give us birth through the word of truth, that we might be a kind of first-fruits of all he created" (v. 18). Therefore, let us cling to the word of truth, the Word of God, to overcome any temptation. This is the very strategy that Jesus Christ used to overcome Satan in the wilderness. Three times he used the Scriptures to defeat Satan in his plot to destroy God's purpose for his life while on earth (cf. Matthew 4:1-11 *et alia*).

God is faithful and will not allow us to be tempted beyond our own strength: "No temptation has overtaken you that is not common to man. God is faithful, and he will not let you be tempted beyond your ability, but with the temptation he will also provide the way of escape, that you may be able to endure it" (1 Corinthians 10:13). But the greatest encouragement we find in the Disciples' Prayer. Our Lord taught us to pray it on a daily basis and the closing of that prayer is certainly the key for a successful day in his presence. He taught us to ask the Father to help us not to fall into temptation. We should come to him and ask, "lead us not into temptation, but deliver us from the evil one" (Matthew 6:13). By going to his throne of grace with this humble petition we are assured that he will provide the deliverance that we need for not falling into temptation.

Chapter 6

Doers of the Word

James 1:19-27

This should be a long chapter, but I believe it is not the size of the message behind it that will determine its content. James, like a poet, is keen in summarizing his thoughts. Here, we see him leading us to the realization that we must live what we believe; and, as we will soon find out, this is only possible if we cling to the Word of God and practice it. For him, faith and praxis go together, there can be no separation of these two concepts. Can we be called the "people of the Book?" How do we relate what we learn in the Bible to what we do in our daily lives? Is there a place for Bible-oriented people in this century of indifference, of materialism and sin? I believe James had those same questions for his flock and this is why his Epistle is so contemporary. We come now to a point where the "word of truth" by which we were created (verse 18), becomes the main factor in our life as Christians. It is because of that word that we are members of the Body of Christ; and this is why we must live a life that is in sync with the True Religion.

We are faced with an invitation to be in agreement with the teachings of the Bible for our lives; if we really want to follow what the Lord has designed for us, we will be quick to hear it and willing to practice it by obeying the Law that gives freedom, the Law of Christ. If we want to be serious about our spiritual journey, which I believe we all are, this is one of the most important passages in the entire

New Testament for us. The world is tired of superficial Christianity; the world is looking for a Church that is strong and honest to the Claims of Jesus Christ. The world is watching the Church to see if we are the true followers of the Savior and Lord Jesus.

Not only that, God is sick of people who come to him with a fake attitude of worship; lip service is a horrendous thing in God's eyes. He is pleased with those who come to him with a service that is spiritual and sincere. The Lord receives the worship of those who have integral lives, people who obey his Word not only with their mouths but also with their hands. This is the core of James teaching at this stage of his Epistle. A summary of the person who lives an integral life is well described in Psalm 1. A quick reading of that Psalm will help us visualize this great reality; but this text is also an important teaching for us so we may be blessed in our walk with the Lord. The highlight of the Psalm is certainly the righteous person's attitude towards the Word of God, "But his delight is in the law of the LORD, and on his law he meditates day and night. He is like a tree planted by streams of water, which yields its fruit in season and whose leaf does not wither. Whatever he does prospers" (Psalm 1:2-3).

How do we live a life that is plentiful and happy? How do we know that God is pleased with our service of worship? How do we show to the world that we are citizens of the Kingdom of God? These and many other questions are answered in how we respond to God's Word. We are ready to learn more about the blessings of the Christian Life as we walk in Word and Deed. The fear that we have, and I will expand on this thought later in this book, is that we may be interfering with God's sovereignty and grace; in fact, deeds do not precede faith. They are the result of a faithful heart. Obedience to God's Word is the result of a strong faith in the God who saves entirely by grace. But the truth is that once we receive that grace and with it the faith we need to be saved, we will respond to the prompting of God in our hearts in order to develop our salvation (cf. Philippians 2:12-13; see also Ephesians 2:10). Our Christian life is not an instant thing; that is, it takes time to be shaped into Jesus' image; it is not a quick fix. Sometimes we are under the illusion that our walk with Jesus is in the fast lane; maybe it is for some, the thief on the cross did not have time to do any good deeds, he was in Heaven, in Paradise with Christ in a matter of a few hours. There are people who come to believe in Jesus in their sick bed and they have time only to be saved; in a few hours, minutes, or days, they are taken to the presence of the Lord, and they are entirely saved. But for most of us, we are called into a life of trials, tribulations, happiness, and so forth; no matter how our life is in the journey set for us, our walk is to be taken one step at a time. James, knowing this very well, encourages us to "be quick to hear, slow to speak, slow to anger" because live goes on and we will learn as we go.

Receiving the Word with Humbleness

There are three basic things to consider for receiving the Word of God in our hearts. First, we need to be quick to listen. It is very common for us to try to have a voice, but it is hard to sit down and listen. To listen is a very difficult art to master. Therefore Jesus Christ has taught his disciples its importance: "Therefore consider carefully how you listen" (Luke 8:18). It is also a matter of knowing him as the Good Shepherd: "My sheep hear my voice, and I know them, and they follow me" (John 10:27). I do not want to over generalize this point but most people who do not listen well are quick judges of others. What I think James is trying to teach in this passage is to call us to pay careful attention to the Word of God. This is a great necessity in our daily life; before we say anything, we must hear what God has to say to us. Sometimes it is very hard for any one to stop and listen if a storm is taking place; we need to be quiet to listen to God's voice at times of affliction. Jeremiah puts it well, after realizing that "the steadfast love of the LORD never ceases" and that "his mercies never come to an end." He goes on to say that "The LORD is good to those who wait for him, to the soul who seeks him. It is good that one should wait quietly for the salvation of the LORD" (Lamentations 3:25-26). I think Jeremiah is here talking about the deliverance that we need during times of trials. The same idea is conveyed by David in Psalms when he wrote, "The salvation of the righteous is from the LORD; he is their stronghold in the time of trouble" (Psalm 37:39). It is paradoxical to suggest that we must be quiet and quick to listen;

but, as we find in the wisdom of James, this is the key to a positive response to God's teaching.

The second basic thing is to be slow to speak; that is, we need to learn how to be slow to react to what we hear. In other words, we must be quick to listen, but take time to think about what our answer will be. A Rabbi once suggested, "Answer a man if you know what to say, but if not, hold your tongue. Honor and shame can come through speaking and a man's tongue may be his downfall." As we will learn in the future (verse 26; 3:1-12), the tongue is the most difficult thing to restrain. One of the things that James is trying to teach us is that if we want to share the Word of God, we better know what we will be talking about.

This also applies to our daily conversation. The Bible is full of teachings about "talking too much." Proverbs has a number of illustrations for us: "When words are many, sin is not absent, but he who holds his tongue is wise" (Proverbs 10:19); "He who guards his lips guards his life, but he who speaks rashly will come to ruin" (Proverbs 13:3); "Do you see a man who speaks in haste? There is more hope for a fool than for him" (Proverbs 29:20).

I have a mark in my old Portuguese Bible, the one I used through my seminary years, which is a reminder of this very truth. It is a small drawing of an angel, strategically put by a given verse that reads, "Set a guard, O LORD, over my mouth; keep watch over the door of my lips!" (Psalm 141:3). It seems embarrassing for me to share the story behind it, but I think it has been a great blessing in my life for many years. It so happened in my last year in seminary, coming close to graduation and I was extremely proud of myself. By that, I must confess, I was critical of everything that was going on around me. In one of our classes, I made some strong remarks about something and felt really good about it; of course, I thought I won that argument. Later that day, I had a small piece of paper given to me by my Professor. The paper was in Hebrew, handwritten and very difficult to decipher. To make things more difficult, it did not have the vowel dots in the text. It took me about two weeks to come up with the translation of that "hieroglyphic" statement. Finally, I got the message through; should I say, I really got the message! It was the above verse, of course. Today, I pray every morning that

The Wisdom Of James

God will set a guard over my mouth so I will not sin against him nor against my fellow pilgrims.

Jesus Christ teaches a wonderful lesson on the issue: "I tell you, on the day of judgment people will give account for every careless word they speak, for by your words you will be justified, and by your words you will be condemned" (Matthew 12:36-37). This is a most humbling teaching from our Lord!

The third thing we learn in this point is that we need to be slow to anger. Anger is the main nest of sin and demonization. Anyone who allows anger to grow in his heart is giving a foothold to the evil one. No prayer will be present in the lives of those who are angry (against God, against others, and against self). There will be no communion among brothers and sisters. There are people who die because they cannot give up their anger. "Man's anger does not bring about the righteous life that God desires." Far from passing folk-psychological words—I think we are saturated with pop psychology already— it has been documented at various levels that people who hold anger inside get sick much easier. Many of them are found in hospitals and wards for mental diseases. The literature and practice of deliverance ministry show that the number of people with demonic problems is also large among those who harbor anger in their hearts.

James is clear in saying that, "the anger of man does not produce the righteousness that God requires." In my experience as an evangelist I have found that this is true not only among people who do not claim to be followers of Jesus, but also among people who call themselves Christians. Unless they are willing to deal with their anger issues, they will not show signs of the Kingdom of God in their lives; by that, I imply the life of righteousness that one will have only through the steady guidance of the Word of God and the assistance of the Holy Spirit. As soon as they choose to deal with their anger, they are open to receive Jesus Christ as their Savior and affirm him as their Lord. You see the difference in their lives. They come up clean, a new joy is visible on their faces; a new life is demonstrated through their actions.

The main step toward a growing life with God is the decision to clean up the house and allow a new reality to take place in our lives. "An uncontrolled tongue and temper drive a man into sin and far from God." We need to put away everything that will allow sin to take over our lives. Anything that will hinder the teaching of God must go. We need to receive the Word of God with humbleness, the Word that is planted in our hearts. We must not resist the teaching of the Word of God. The *English Standard Version* reads, "receive with meekness the implanted word, which is able to save your souls" (v. 21b).

Putting the Word of God into Practice

This is the hard part of it: To put into practice what God is trying to teach us through his Word. Sometimes it is too easy to go to church and just hear what the preacher has to say. Most of the members of any church won't remember even the text of the message that was preached in the Sunday morning service. This is not a negative remark, it is the plain reality of things. We are easily distracted and forgetful; we come from a culture that is very hard to remember things. Even when we take notes of all we hear, we usually do not even remember where we stacked those notes for further reference. People from oral traditional cultures have the amazing gift of remembering things. The contrast can be seen also with our singing in church: We sing the same hymns for many years and few of us remember the words of those hymns—I am included in this group. If we do not have the hymnals, chorus books, or the PowerPoint screen in front of us, we will hum and come up with just a few words or verses. I had the privilege of having a student from Ghana in one of my Mission courses a few years ago. A number of people, including me, noticed that he did not bring any notebook to class; he did not even open the syllabus to follow the outline of my classes. That, of course, disturbed me and a few of his classmates. He was, however, a straight A student. We learned later that he came from an oral culture and he retained all the teaching by hearing; he was able to memorize the entire class teaching and reproduce it later in his own words either in a written paper or when taking an oral exam. Without any exaggeration, I submit that we should aim to retain the Word of God in our hearts and keep it by heart. No matter what process we have in our minds to retain the Word, the Holy Spirit will use for our benefit.

The key of James teaching here is to draw his audience to the uncomfortable reality of becoming doers of the Word, not hearers only. He expands this very idea when he addresses various issues related to our Christian living: not showing partiality, helping the poor and the needy, taming our tongue, living lives that show God's holiness, doing justice, being patience, trusting the Lord with our future, being patience, and exercising our faith through prayer. These are just a few things that he covers, but whose principles are applied to live as a whole. The point is clear: Walk the talk! Do what you believe! Practice what you learn! There is no room for a theoretical life with Jesus Christ; for him, theory leads to praxis.

There are a few considerations that I want to share with you at this stage: The first is about *obedience*. The Lord has more pleasure in obedience than in aimless sacrifices. The illustration of the mirror shows us the importance of the Word of God. It will prepare our hearts to understand the role of the *Perfect Law* in our lives. The Bible is the true mirror that will show us who we really are. Even though a mirror did not shine as clear then as it does today—it is also an instrument from outside our own sensory experience—and does not present any sign of change; the Bible is clear, shows our inner beings with clarity, and produces permanent change in our lives.

The call of this text is for us to get involved, to do something! *Get Involved!* is the message for us who are called to be doers of the Word. That is why Jesus will come with a hard question in that glorious day: "Why do you call me 'Lord, Lord,' and do not do what I tell you?" (Luke 6:46).

Sharing Our Lives Under the Word

The result of listening to the Word of God and doing what it teaches is easy to grasp: "he will be blessed in what he does." Even under some trials and temptations, the doers of the Word will enjoy blessings from above. This is different from what the Theology of Prosperity has to offer. The blessings that come from obedience will be shown in many different ways, not in materialist or carnal; that is, fleshly terms only.

The way we bridle our tongue will show what we do. This truth leads to an important sequence of actions in the closing of this first chapter. There are three aspects of this sharing of our lives in the world: As a matter of evangelism, we share the Truth of God. Measuring the words that will come out of our mouths; which, in fact, is another way of showing our self-control, will open the doors for others to hear the Good News of the Kingdom. Second, we share our lives under the Word of God by serving our neighbors through our "personal ministry to the human need" (v. 27). Thirdly, by showing to the world that we live a life of holiness, an undefiled life with God.

Our lives are living letters when we are obedient to the Word of God. James' conclusion of this teaching points to three important behavioral outcomes for those who are doers of the Word. First, they need to control their speech; he simply points out that, "If anyone thinks he is religious and does not bridle his tongue but deceives his heart, this person's religion is worthless" (v. 26). He will deal with this particular problem we all face later. But we need to once again remind ourselves that our tongue is sometimes a wild beast.

Now, looking from a different angle, the use of our speech is instrumental for the spread of our faith. From this perspective the way we live our lives under the Word of God is the best means of evangelism and mission in a time when the world want to see what we are as Christian people. It is interesting how James links the doing of the Word with how we use our tongues (v. 26). In so many ways, it is our tongue that will tell the world what we really believe and who we really are. How we tame our tongue will reveal the real self in each of us. Jesus Christ taught his disciples this important truth when he said, " For out of the abundance of the heart the mouth speaks" (Matthew 12:34b). Here we have something important to keep in mind: our attitude towards life will be demonstrated by what we speak. If our religion is centered in the Word of God, our behavior will reflect what we say.

The second aspect of this behavior is as important as the first. Our lives do not convey who we really are through words only, but also through our actions. This seems to be a repetitious rhetoric but it is necessary at this point. There is a tremendous burden in James' heart for those who are suffering. Here we reemphasize the compassionate heart of God through his teaching. Not only we must speak what we believe, but we must act on it. The True Religion is defined by what we do, much more than by what we say. The believer is expected to show compassion towards the powerless. The orphan and the widow are visible illustrations of powerlessness, which is the worst description of poverty. James is not advocating any form of "social gospel"; rather, he is in perfect line with the teaching of the Old Testament and of the Lord Jesus Christ. He is not setting any political agenda, no Liberation Theology; rather, he is defining the behavior of the Kingdom of God and its values. This is a humbling reminder to the Church of the wholeness of Mission; the missionary nature of the Church must be complete. It must be in Word and in Deed. Each and every believer is in his or her own way a missionary par excellence. Every time we reflect the values of the Kingdom of God we are proclaiming the Good News of the Kingdom; be they in Word or in Deed. Here, James clearly levels the balance between Evangelism, which is taken by many as sharing the Word in words, and Social Responsibility, which is sharing the Word in action.

The third aspect of this behavior has to do with holiness and sanctity of life. This is also a key behavioral aspect of the True Religion. Without being judgmental, we see a number of people doing good deeds because of their consciences. I do not need to delve into this issue at the moment; we see it happening in many different forms and shapes. What makes the difference here is that the believer worships the Lord in truth and in spirit, but before it takes place, they have been regenerated by the Holy Spirit; in other words, they are found guiltless before the throne of God. The mission of the Church is based on the result of redeemed hearts serving a Holy God. But we know that we believers struggle with trials and temptations. That is why James reminds us that True Religion is holy. Therefore, we are commanded to keep ourselves unstained by the world. Our sanctified lives will show that we are true believers.

When we live a life that is under trials and temptations, we must cling to the Word of God with a humble attitude. We must be quick

The Wisdom Of James

to listen, slow to answer, and in all we must live lives that show that the Lord is in control of our hearts, minds, soul and spirit through his Word. We are called to grow in the Word of Truth, the Word that gave us life, with humbleness, obedience, and ministry to others.

I cannot help but turn to the teaching of Jesus Christ at this point. James seems to be reminding his audience of Jesus' teaching about the tree and its fruit and also about the wise builders in the Sermon on the Mount. About the tree, he says, "every healthy tree bears good fruit" (Matthew 7:17a) and about the wise builders, he says, "Everyone then who hears these words of mine and does them will be like a wise man who built his house on the rock. And the rain fell, and the floods came, and the winds blew and beat on that house, but it did not fall, because it had been founded on the rock" (Matthew 7:24-25).

Chapter 7

Faith and Law: The Test of Love

James 2:1-13

I am not unmindful, as a Southerner, of the force of this virus of prejudice. I know, however, that there is a cure for this virus, and that is our faith. As pastor of your souls, I am happy to take the responsibility for any evil which might result from different races worshiping God together, but I would be unwilling to take the responsibility of those who refuse to worship God with a person of another race. (Bishop V. S. Waters)

The Epistle of James is made up of a series of tests, all of them related to our faith. The first chapter deals the test of our faith through many trials and temptations. In fact, the major test is that one of our faith. As we continue to read the epistle, however, we will soon realize that when we are tested in our faith, we are also being tested in several key areas of our Christian life. Right now we face a humbling test in our faith: the test of love. This is a very sobering passage. It deals with our faith in a new perspective. The second chapter of James deals with the test of *love in action*. It is here that we stop to think about our attitude toward others in two significant ways: how we relate with our neighbor in a loving way and, later, how we demonstrate our faith through the deeds that we are expected to produce.

The Wisdom Of James

The first part of the second chapter of James brings us to a point of contrition; but, before it takes place, a key question must be raised: How can I fulfill the law by faith only? It is interesting to note that the Author is here introducing the issue of Law and Faith so that we be aware of what will come next: Our Justification by Faith is vindicated by our actions, by our deeds. As we explore this passage, we will realize that it is full of contrasts, mostly between types of personal and corporate preferences: poor vs. rich, faith vs. law, love vs. discrimination, judgment vs. mercy. This passage is key in our understanding of grace and legalism; but, also, it is a key teaching from James on how we fulfill the Royal Law, the Law of Love, the Law that brings freedom (cf. 1:25).

The time when this chapter was delivered in the form of a sermon, we were under the horrifying news about the two major hurricanes that hit the south of the United States, Katrina and Rita. During that time, the issue of racism and social preference came up again and again. It was like touching a sore wound that had never been treated before, even forty years after the climax of the social changes had began in that part of the country. Much good has been shown after the Katrina and Rita devastation; we see that people from all over the nation—as well as from many other nations—have stepped out to provide help and share with the suffering of those who lost everything. By addressing this teaching now, we are reminded once more that we will be known as Christians by the quality of life that we live: a life that shows no partiality, a life that reflects the love of Jesus Christ in and through us.

It is in a time like this that the Church of Jesus Christ is called to go through the crucible and be tested in its love quality. The test of love is here presented to us without any political correctness or any other preconceived agenda. It is the essence of the Christian ethic; it is the clear teaching of the Law of Christ, the Law of Love.

Seek No Favoritism

The center of this teaching is clearly stated: *Remove discrimination from your lives*. Although this is a negative statement, it is necessary for us to deal with the issue of discrimination and favor-

80

itism. There is no room for such an attitude among us Christians. James is very clear in that statement: We share the faith of our Lord Jesus Christ, the Lord of Glory. We must grasp the depth of this proposition from James: "Faith of Jesus Christ" is in the genitive; it is a faith that comes from Jesus Christ Himself. It originates in him and is given to us by God's grace. A commentator put it this way, **"The Faith of our Lord Jesus Christ** is not compatible with such partiality. To discriminate between persons because of their social or financial status is to pass judgments from evil motives, to **become judges with evil thoughts**. Life according to the Christian faith and life according to worldly standards are in sharp contrast here. The faith which originates in Jesus Christ disavows distinctions based upon birth, race, property, or sex (cf. Gal. 3:28)."

The Greek word for "favoritism," or "partiality" literally means "to receive the face." It means to estimate people by their superficial appearance, rather than on the basis of their inner personality, as a commentator puts well, "on the basis of their fundamental humanity." James is teaching us to look to others from a different perspective, not based on other people's outward appearance; rather, upon their heart.

The supreme example for us is Jesus Christ Himself, who sat with the rich and the poor; he ate with the Pharisees, but also received the honor from a prostitute. He talked with the powerful, but gave his time to the poor. In fact, he came to preach the Good News of the Kingdom to the poor (Luke 4:18-20; 7:22). Our God does not show partiality (Romans 2:11; Acts 10:34; Ephesians 6:9). When we pray the Lord's Prayer together, we all come to the Lord as equals: "Our Father..." There are many illustrations of how sinful discrimination is, but I will attain to just few that I think would help us grasp the concept.

I remember being in a bus station in Brasília some thirty years ago. It was the [Brazilian] Independence Day and I had to travel to that city in order to get another bus to my home town. We were waiting for the bus in a long line, tired and hungry. There was an old Italian man begging for some change in order to pay his fare in that same bus. Most of us pitched in and he was able to pay for his ticket. As soon as we boarded, that man started to mistreat a

81

The Wisdom Of James

lady with her infant in her arms. The man wanted to have the front seat, which was assigned to that woman. He continued in his broken Portuguese to say demeaning words to the woman, demanding that she would leave and grab a seat in the back of the bus. It took a few of us passengers to stand up and go talk with that man. I remember one of us saying to him that he should not be mistreating anybody, and that that woman, although poor, was one of those who actually helped pay for his bus fare. The man, in his pride, had the notion, and he spoke about that to everybody, that because he was European he had the right to ride in the front seat. After a moment of tension, we had the bus driver to come and tell the man he should sit in his assigned seat in the back of the bus.

I speak for those who, like me, come from a different cultural background at this time. It has been my experience in some occasions to be treated differently just because I have an English (or Portuguese) accent. I am not only talking about being misunderstood or turned down in the market place; I am also talking about sometimes being mistreated in the church. In the market place, having lived in Southern California for so many years, it was common to be treated unfairly by a number of people: in shopping malls, in the school system, in the airports, and so on. It has been more difficult to be different in appearance and having an accent in the airports after 9/11, however. I always carry with me a photocopy of my American passport, just in case. Sometimes it is actually fun to live like this! In many occasions in the past, while traveling nationwide on church and mission related business, I faced people who did not even think I was able to communicate well in English. There have been churches where people would speak with me very slowly and loud so I could understand better, they would think; others would say that they did not have any Spanish-speaking congregation in their building so I could worship there or that there was not any Hispanic Pastor whom to talk. Later, I would have a chance to introduce myself, usually by handing them my business card, just to see how they reacted. Of course I never did that on purpose, but it has been somewhat fun to see how uncomfortable and embarrassed some would be.

When I was in seminary back in Brazil, I had a conversation with an American mission bureaucrat about the possibility of becoming a pastor in the United States someday. He was gracious and open to the idea. Actually his denomination had at that time just entered into an agreement with my denomination to provide the best venues for that to happen. The deal was in these lines: If an American missionary wanted to minister in a Brazilian church, all he had to do was to learn Portuguese and then have full positions in any church that might need a pastor. If a Brazilian wanted to serve in the United States, they would find a Hispanic congregation (it would be better if they found a Brazilian fellowship or mission church) for him to serve. I asked why a Brazilian could not serve in an American congregation. He told me that we Brazilians were not prepared well enough to minister in an American Church. I proved him wrong, as have many Hispanics, Arabs (from Egypt, Sudan, Lebanon), Brazilians, and other brothers and sisters from many different cultures around the globe. In my case, I have been blessed with the opportunity to serve only in both Native American and All-American Churches in the United States.

Mahatma Gandhi, who was not a Christian, went to a church to see and hear his good friend C. F. Wells in South Africa. He was turned away because of the color of his skin. The interesting thing to note here, besides that unloving incident, is that Gandhi fought against the caste system in his native India. An Italian missionary in a mission work in America had this to say of the wealthy American congregation that supported him and his ministry: "They want us to be saved, but they don't want to associate with us."

Leonardo was a dear friend of mine in seminary. He chose to minister among the prostitutes in the Old Recife, the red light section of metropolitan Recife, in Northeast Brazil. He was blessed with the gift of evangelism and led a good number of prostitutes to Christ. Many of them had never lived anywhere else but that place. Old Recife is known to be a prostitution place where mothers introduce their daughters to their customers; children grow in that place with a culture of sex, alcohol, and drugs as their natural habitat. Some of those women who came to Christ did not know any other lifestyle but the one they grew up in. It is a subculture of sin and depravation. When they became our sisters in Christ, Leo provided follow up and discipleship to them. But they could not find a new place to live, although they wanted to leave that life and follow Jesus. I remember one evening when Leo came back to our dorm with tears in his eyes. It was about "Lúcia," a young woman who had become a disciple of Jesus. Her faith was growing strong and she had quit selling herself. But there was no place for her, no skills, no job, no shelter. When she was forced to work by her Madam, she refused and tried to evangelize the other woman. Lúcia was found murdered and half buried in a shallow ditch not far from the place she used to live. I remember Leo's comment to me saying that the church at large did not want to receive a former prostitute as a new member. This reminded me of the parable of the ten virgins in Matthew 25. I still believe that those women became virgins by the grace of God. In Jesus Christ they were completely healed from their sins and, like Lúcia, they were called virgins, the symbol of purity. This is the kind of prejudice, the kind of discrimination that we unfortunately see in the Church. This is what James was adamantly against in his Epistle.

Realize the Richness of Faith

Now James brings forth an even more dramatic illustration of how the Christians were showing partiality. He uses the illustration of the poor and the rich. By doing so, he also shows the treatment that God has towards the poor. It is very easy to understand that someone would love the rich and famous; but not the poor and downtrodden. The Bible shows that God never forsakes the poor. As an example, we go to the mission statement of Jesus Christ Himself. "The Spirit of the Lord is upon me, because he has anointed me to proclaim good news to the poor. He has sent me to proclaim liberty to the captives and recovering of sight to the blind, to set at liberty those who are oppressed, to proclaim the year of the Lord's favor" (Luke 4:18-19; cf. Isaiah 61:1-3).

Again, I should mention that discrimination is a *cancer* in the Body of Christ. By discriminating against others, we are building up a wall among ourselves: "have you not made distinction among yourselves?" (vs. 4). We need to bear in mind that in Jesus Christ we are all made one. Christ gives us dignity and equality through his blood on the Cross.

A word should be said about the poor, even so briefly. The Lord has a special attention to the needs of the poor throughout the Bible. He is the Father of the fatherless, the Husband of the widows. We may have heard from advocates of the Social Gospel, from Liberation Theology theoreticians, from liberal theologians that God has a preference for the poor. I disagree with that statement, but at the same time I completely agree with God's position toward the poor and downtrodden. He has a special attention to their needs. This is indisputable in the Word; nobody who is able to read and interpret the Holy Scriptures can say that God does not have that special attachment to those in dire straits. A great illustration, among hundreds in the Bible, is the beautiful story of Ruth and Naomi. It depicts the intent of God in showing the relationship between their poverty and our need of redemption. The Lord has constantly shown that the poor are the objects of his love and providence.

At the same token, God dispenses his grace to the rich. The very fact that James deals with the rich in this Epistle demonstrates that rich people are also included in God's plan of salvation. There are numerous illustrations of rich people who have been saved in the Bible; some of them became rich which is the case of Abram, Jacob, Joseph of Egypt, King David. Barnabas was a rich man who, later, sold some of his properties to help the poor. Paul grew up in a wealthy family from Tarsus; his father was a wealthy tradesman. Moreover, Paul had good relationship with wealthy people during his missionary work; many of them opened their homes for the Church—we should be reminded that the Early Church used to meet in homes in many instances (e.g.: Acts 20; Romans 16). We must consider poverty in two categories in the New Testament teaching of Jesus: First there are the poor in spirit (Matthew 5:3). I understand it to be a little bit like this: There is a number of rich people who are totally poor spiritually (I must make clear that Jesus was not directing himself to rich only, of course). But Jesus also speaks of the plain poor with more emphasis than in Matthew in the way Luke recorded his teaching on the Mount and elsewhere (Luke 4:18-19; cf. Luke 6:20, 7:22). I also understand that there are many poor

The Wisdom Of James

people who are spiritually rich. This is the paradox of the Christian Faith. It is all related to the values of the Kingdom of God.

The Kingdom of God is, as a Christian sociologist once pointed out, an "upside-down kingdom." The Lord brings people to the same level: He brings the rich down, He lifts the poor up (James 1:9-10). Therefore, James continues to say that the poor of this world are the rich in faith. What he says about the rich is very humbling. We are not sure whether he is talking about some rich Christians who were still acting as former Jewish citizens (as they did in the courts) or whether he was talking about the rich visitors who were not believers yet. No matter what James had in mind, the application is very clear. We are saved to be rich in faith! We all will inherit the Kingdom with Christ. But Jesus often made mention of this truth as a special comfort for the poor. "Blessed are you who are poor, for yours is the kingdom of God" (Luke 6:20).

But our poverty will profit into great richness. The Kingdom of God makes us all rich, not destitute. Every single person who enters the Kingdom of God must enter it as a pauper. This is the requirement of Jesus to the young rich ruler: Our poverty is translated into total surrender to Jesus Christ, total loss of whatever we consider our greatest asset or possession. We must move from possessors to possessed; from proprietors to property. Jesus Christ bought us with a price; therefore, we do not have anything to show as our possession, we are his possession (cf. 1 Corinthians 6:19b-20). Our wealth is our inheritance in the Kingdom. We are heirs with Christ and this is what makes us all rich in God's sight. We should be always reminded that the end of History will disclose this very truth to the entire universe. It will be in that glorious day that we will all see who is who, who will have made the Lord's top 500, if I may use such a language. It will be the day when we will hear the Lord say, "Come, you who are blessed by my Father; take your inheritance, the kingdom prepared for you since the creation of the world" (Matthew 25:34).

Keep the Royal Law

James is expecting that his readers will mention something about the Law and its rewards. But before they do so, he introduces a new interpretation of what is not to show favoritism. The opposite of favoritism (prejudice, discrimination) is *love*. Therefore, he brings forth the Law of Jesus Christ, what he calls the Royal Law: "You shall love your neighbor as yourself." Again, he comes up with a new illustration, this time a theological one. The theological problem is posed before them: *If*. If someone keeps the whole law but fails in just one point of it, that person will fail miserably in the test of love. Here he is showing that partiality is a sin according to the Law of Moses: he draws his line of thought from the Scripture, from the book of Leviticus. One of the pressing passages is related to how we should treat the poor, "You shall do no injustice in court. You shall not be partial to the poor or defer to the great, but in righteousness shall you judge your neighbor" (Lev. 19:15). Another version renders it, "Do not pervert justice; do not show partiality to the poor or favoritism to the great, but judge your neighbor fairly." He then links that portion of the Law to the teaching of Jesus, who also quoted Leviticus, "you shall love your neighbor as yourself" (Matthew 22:39; cf. Leviticus 19:18b). Here, James is in complete harmony with the teaching of Jesus Christ. That is why he calls it the Royal Law.

James is a master in offering extreme illustrations. He then takes "to kill," "to commit murder" and "to show partiality," comparing them as the same thing. He is using a Hebrew parallelism by doing so in verse 11. James makes this dramatic comparison to show the seriousness of the issue he is talking about. By obeying the Law of the King, we are fulfilling the second greatest commandment. *Love is the key to fight discrimination.* He adds to this illustration a great point of reference for our journey: by obeying the Law of Love we will truly be free, because the Royal Law is also the Law of Liberty.

Our prejudices are normal expressions of our personal fears. We are constantly entrapped in the vicious habit of comparing ourselves with others. Different people frighten us. I often tell my students

The Wisdom Of James

that we all, including me, have our prejudices at a certain level. You may disagree with this statement at this moment, but I would like to invite you to search your heart with the help of the Holy Spirit in order to find what kind of prejudice you have. This is the prison cage where we find ourselves in and out. It never stops. When we overcome one kind of prejudice, we will be lured into another trap, which could be even bigger than the first. Let me illustrate this in a more general way, trying not to be too judgmental, of course. Take the entertainment industry for example. I remember growing up with some old cartoons that would show the bad guys with a heavy German accent. Then the bad guys suddenly had a Russian (Soviet) accent or were named Boris, Ivan, whatever name that would reflect the Cold War. Not long ago, most bad guys were from South America: they came from some countries with funny names (to hide the real ones: Colombia, Cuba, etc.) and their names were all Hispanic and had the Hispanic accent. You got my point. Today, we are growing fast in our prejudices against anybody with a Middle Eastern resemblance, which goes with the historical development of the past sixty or so years: Germans were linked with the Second World War; Soviets with KGB and Communism; Hispanics with the drug war, mostly coming from Colombia; and now the surge of terrorism worldwide has made us clearly "afraid" of anybody who looks like a Middle Eastern person. This is our constant prison; the fear of others. As a result, we are prone to discriminate, to make distinction between one person and another. Phobia is the term that best describes our root of discrimination. We as a Church are afraid of evangelizing the poor without realizing that the United States poverty level is increasing very fast in its grass roots; we are afraid of getting involved with HIV/AIDS victims because we cannot see that it has become a world pandemic. Our legalistic prejudice is very high in that level. We avoid getting involved in social and political action because we are afraid of being labeled as liberals, communists, or plain Democrats.

The Royal Law is the ticket to freedom. It is the Law of Love that has been taught by the Lord Jesus that will set us free from our prejudices. With the love that comes from the Holy Spirit, we will be free and will not walk in fear any more, this is the basic teaching of John the Apostle. God is love and love casts away all fear (cf. 1 John 4:7-10). James is trying to teach us this wonderful truth; that, although we are prone to have our pet prejudices, it is by obeying the Law of Love, the Royal Law that we will be completely free.

Show Mercy, Not Judgment!

This is the summary of James' teaching at this point in his Epistle. It is the triumph of love over favoritism, partiality, and discrimination. Here is how to do it: *"Speak and Act!"* He puts it in very practical terms, "So speak and so act as those who are to be judged under the law of liberty" (vs. 12). I am confident to suggest that what he means in this verse is simply this: "put in practice what you speak." Live according to what you believe because the love you have in your heart comes from Jesus Christ in the same way your faith comes from him. Have a Christian life that really shows that you abide by the Law of Christ.

He has also a sobering admonition to his readers that closely deals with the final judgment from the Lord. God is the only Judge. Therefore, we need to act as those who are to be judged under the Law of Liberty, the Law that brings forth freedom (1:25). All of us will stand before the Judge in the Day of the Lord. At the same time, he adds that mercy triumphs over judgment. To show mercy is the way we will triumph over judgment. By doing so we are declaring to the world that we are a community of forgiven people. This reminds me of the story of the man who was forgiven his enormous debt and then did not forgive his debtor (cf. Matthew 18:21-35). Again, James has Jesus' teaching on forgiveness which is intrinsically related to the issue of mercy. After all, it was God's mercy that kept us alive until the day we accepted Jesus Christ as our Savior and Lord. If the Lord had such a mercy toward us, we should have mercy toward our neighbor.

We have a tremendous challenge before us as a Church in this time of so much confusion and hatred. What surrounds us is trying to mold us every day. The world has a pattern that tries to dictate its agenda on the Church. At the time of this writing we are celebrating the 100th anniversary of the birth of a man who did not allow the forces of this age to determine his faith. I am talking about Dietrich Bohnoeffer. A German pastor who had the courage of not succumbing to the craziness of Adolf Hitler. While the institutionalized church in Germany was approving the rise of the Third Reich, he and other men and women decided to pay the ultimate price. Describing who he was, a Christian magazine put it this way, "[he was] the young German theologian who offered one of the few clear voices of resistance to Adolf Hitler and the rise of the Nazis. He challenged the church to stand with the Jews in their time of need. . . . he was executed by the Nazis just weeks before the end of the war. He was 39."

I believe James was a non-conformist in his time. He had a clear view of what Jesus Christ taught his disciples and acted upon it. Speaking as a prophet, he had the courage to obey the prompting of the Holy Spirit and write these words that are so eloquent and necessary even for our present day. We should not discriminate, we should love those who are different from us. We should seek the heart of God and love those whom God has poured his own life on their behalf through the sacrifice of his Son Jesus Christ. In times like these, we should overcome our pitiful sense of self-righteousness and engage in a more merciful and loving agenda both within the church and out in the world. Unless the world sees that we have a genuine love, the one that comes from God, in our hearts, we will not make a difference in this age. May the Lord have mercy on us!

Chapter 8

Faith and Deeds: The Test of Orthodoxy

James 2:14-26

Christ can do without your works; what he wants is you. Yet if he really has you, he will have all your works. (F. T. Forsyth)

A man of words and not of deeds is like a garden full of weeds. (Anonymous)

One of our misunderstandings about the right doctrine is that most of the time we do not pay attention to the importance of the right praxis as well. Let me explain: Sound doctrine is always accompanied by sound responsive acts to that doctrine. This is a key element in our faith. As we continue to explore this series of various tests, we come now to the test of our orthodoxy; that is, the test of our faith as it relates to what we claim to believe. In our case, I would like to suggest that James is concerned with what we do to demonstrate our view of Justification. Before I move on, I think a question is now in order: What is orthodoxy in the Christian Faith? I understand it to be the locus of our belief system; again, it is the canon that we use to measure what we believe, according to what is taught in the Holy Scriptures, and also to be validated through the acts of that same faith, according to the deeds that we show in response to that confession.

No matter what denominational or non-denominational background we have, you and I belong to a Church that is confessional. The Church of Jesus Christ spread around the world and throughout the ages is in itself a confessional entity. The very reason of each of us having to confess Jesus Christ as our Lord and Savior proves it. There are churches, however, that have a body of confession or confessions. I come from a Reformed and Evangelical background; in my case, for instance, I confess Jesus Christ according to the teachings of the Scripture; but also I subscribe to at least two creeds, one confession, and another worldwide statement of Evangelical Faith. I subscribe to the Apostles' Creed and to the Nicene Creed, but also to the Westminster Confession of Faith and to the articles of faith of the Lausanne Fellowship, presented to the world in 1974. This brings to the reality that we have statements of our faith that we subscribe in our diverse traditions. I might say, nonetheless, that any creed, confession of faith, and related documents, are imperfect and incomplete; the Bible is the only canon by which we measure our faith. In this case, the Holy Scripture is the only rule of faith and practice for any Christian who honestly wants to follow and obey the Lord Jesus Christ.

This is a very secure way to deal with what we call "orthodoxy." In a nutshell, orthodoxy can be translated simply as the right doctrine. The word is composed of two others (*ortho* and *doxy*). *Ortho* means straight, correct, proper. It is used in other known terms such orthodontics, orthopedics, and orthography. The second word is related to the Greek term *doxa*, which means "opinion." Another term should be introduced at this point, "orthopraxy." It should be translated as the right practice. Thus, James is trying to teach his audience that Pure Religion (Orthodoxy) is known to others through True Praxis (Orthopraxy).

Before I move on, I am aware of other orthodoxies in Christian Faith. I am not suggesting that they do not claim to have the right doctrine. The fact that we belong to a kaleidoscope of different worldviews, customs, cultures, and so forth, makes clear that all those aspects of life and culture will affect how we call ourselves to be orthodox in our approach to our faith. Granted, I must say that what was once very unorthodox became mainline, or mainstream, in many aspects later. The tools and the way one person has to interpret the Scripture will certainly determine her or his level of orthodoxy. In my case, however, I claim my orthodoxy based on what the Scripture has taught over the span of more than two thousand years of agreement on issues that are considered to be essentials to the Christian Faith. Those essentials are present in the confession of the Evangelical Christians spread around the world.

This portion of James is the soil for many a debate between the issue of Justification by Faith alone (Sola Fide) and Justification by Works. Martin Luther, for example, considered this letter to be spurious because he could not reconcile the two perceptions of Justification, not being able to grasp the intention of James; that is, his theological intention for this letter. Apparently, there seems to be a contradiction between what Paul and James are saying about faith (i.e., Paul in Romans and James in his letter). We do not know whether Paul is trying to solve the problem that James had touched before (remember that the Epistle of James was written prior to Paul's letter to the Romans). I believe that both were not in disagreement, fighting for one side or the other; rather, I have a strong sense that it was the prompting of the Holy Spirit in trying to show us that there are two ways we see Justification. One, from a vertical point of view, presented by the Apostle Paul in Romans, and the other, from a horizontal point of view, in this passage of James.

Another word that I want to add to this apparent controversy is related to a number of confronting ideas that will bring to us a better understanding of what it is to have a genuine faith. This text will prompt us to compare the uselessness of faith in some areas that we necessarily do not want to touch, such as hypocrisy, self-righteousness, and also the huge issue of nominalism in contemporary Christianity. We see two extremes that are coded as left and right in this present age. The ultra-orthodox or Fundamentalists who go to the extreme right and play a great disfavor to the spread of the Gospel; but also the left wing which have for long broadened the gap between praxis and orthodoxy. They also have done much damage to the Gospel. In one sense, the extreme left wing is as Fundamentalist

The Wisdom Of James

as the extreme right. I believe that this passage is the bonding glue that will bring both orthodoxy and orthopraxy together; this is what has been intended by God from the beginning.

Another issue that I want to bring to the fore at this time has to do with the issue of knowing who is who in the faith. I want also to say that it is impossible to know for sure whether someone is a saved person or not. Only God Himself knows his elect. But there are some instances in the Bible that give us ways of knowing if someone's faith is genuine or not. Out of several Scripture readings, I find these to be solid arguments in favor of what I am trying to say: In Matthew 7:17-20, we read, "Likewise every good tree bears good fruit, but a bad tree bears bad fruit. A good tree cannot bear a bad fruit, and a bad tree cannot bear good fruit. Every tree that does not bear good fruit is cut down and thrown into the fire. Thus, by their fruit you will recognize them." Also, we read in 2 Corinthians that there is a radical transformation in the lives of those who become followers of Jesus Christ through faith. Paul writes that, "Therefore, if anyone is in Christ, he is a new creation; the old has gone, the new has come!" (2 Corinthians 5:17). But there is yet a more striking passage in Paul's writing that I would like to point out. He gives us a clear understanding that we have the need sometimes to check on our own orthodoxy. Again, writing to the problematic church in Corinth, he gives this impression when he writes that we should test ourselves whether we are in Christ or not, "Examine yourselves to see whether you are in the faith; test yourselves. Do you not realize that Christ Jesus is in you—unless, of course, you fail the test?" (2 Corinthians 13:5). The last word of this verse is entirely linked to the issue of orthodoxy; in fact, the very verb "to test" yourselves is from the same stem. Both words, the verb and the noun are from the stem *doxa*. For Paul, "to fail the test" means to be outside the doctrine; that is, to be outside the *doxa*. Therefore, we are not in the business of judging others, which is easily done according to the morality of the person; but we are commanded by the Word of God to test ourselves whether we are in the doctrine or not; whether we are in Christ Jesus or not. For Paul, and I believe for James as well, this is one and the same thing. That is the reason for our test of orthodoxy.

The Spurious Faith

We must deal with the spurious faith at this point. What makes faith spurious? I am amazed how the word "faith" has been misused in the thinking of many people. In my first culture, it is used in so many different ways that it is even hard to try to come up with a clear view of what it really means. *Faith* in Portuguese is *fé*; along with it we have another quantitative rendering of the word, it is sometimes used in the diminutive, which is a common usage in Portuguese to designate something that is either unimportant or, if related to people, a sentimental form of care. In the case of faith, Brazilians use it sometimes as *fezinha*, little faith. So, when someone calls a bookie to place a bet, they will say, "I'll put a fezinha" on this number, or game, or whatever it is—soccer game, horse derbies, lottery, and so on. But also, we see a number of people who put their faith on any kind of deities, *orixás* (Afro-Brazilian spiritual entities), saints, and the list grows bigger with other options. But I thought this was a phenomenon that occurred only in my native Brazil. Was I wrong! I see it happening almost daily in the North America as well, it does not matter if I am in Canada, United States, or in Mexico. Or even among Native Americans or First Nations people. Their faith is as fluid as it is in Brazil. The issue is not a New World (Continental America) case only; it is worldwide. Then we move to other regions of the world and find spurious faith everywhere. This comes wrapped in our own sinful state. It is a remarkable and common problem that we all share, including in the Church. Yes, there is spurious faith in the Church as well!

According to James, a spurious faith is demonstrated in four negative characteristics, all of them interlinked. A spurious faith is: devoid of deeds, ineffective towards God, lacking in obedience and lacking in courage. Three times he shows the seriousness of faith when it is not genuine: It is *dead* (v. 17), it is *useless* (v. 20); and, again, it is *dead* (v. 26). Talking about a *dead faith*, we will find out that it is in itself lifeless and it cannot generate anything, either good or bad. A dead thing does not produce anything by its own configuration; that is, it does not bear any fruit.

The Wisdom Of James

There are three ways we can see how faith is dead. First, a faith that lacks compassion for the others will prove to be dead. Faith is closely related to action. "Faith by itself, if it is not accompanied by action is dead (2:17)." Again, James makes a statement with a profound impact on anyone who reads his Epistle, "Can that faith save him?" This is a most important question to ask because we are saved by faith and by faith only. But there is no contradiction with the teaching of the Scripture. If we go to Paul and John, for example, they also bring forth the same reality of faith being demonstrated by our actions. One of the key texts to illustrate this is found in Paul's letter to the Ephesians (2:8-9). We are quick to state our orthodoxy by quoting it. Not only does that text affirm what we believe—remember, we are confessional—but also, it seems to give us that sense of not having to do anything else. In fact, we cannot do anything to be saved, we cannot add anything toward our salvation. Salvation is indeed by grace through faith. But we seem to not read the one verse that comes after that, which is intrinsically and completely linked with our salvation, "For we are his workmanship, created in Christ Jesus *for good works*, which God prepared beforehand, that we should walk in them" (Ephesians 2:10, emphasis added). Here we see the principle of the good tree that Jesus was referring to in the Sermon on the Mount. The Apostle John uses a similar argument when he talks about our integrity of faith. The question behind his argument is obvious: How do we know what love is? He links it with the same issue of love in action, "By this we know love, that he laid down his life for us, and we ought to lay down our lives for our brothers. But if anyone has the world's goods and sees his brother in need, yet closes his heart against him, how does God's love abide in him? Little children, let us not love in word or talk but in deed and in truth" (1 John 2:16-18).

A faith which lacks evidence of deeds is barren. It is mere religiosity, void of life. This is something to think about. That is why James makes a comment about the faith of demons. John Bristol, a Presbyterian minister, once put it this way in a message on this very text,

James keeps up with his dialog with the person who claims to have faith but has no deeds to prove it. . . . He writes in verse 19: "You believe there is a God. Good! Even the demons believe that—and shudder." James wanted to shock his complacent readers so he uses demons for an illustration. Intellectual assent to correct doctrine is not the same as saving faith. The fact is even demons believe there is one God. In Luke 8:28 we read that demons who had possessed the man of Gadara shrieked out at Jesus, "What have we to do with you, Jesus, Son of the Most High God?" They knew who Jesus was. It has been said that the devil himself is perfectly orthodox in his theology. Now it is good to have orthodox theology. It is right to believe there is one God. Monotheism is better than polytheism. James acknowledges this when he writes, "You believe that there is one God. Good!" This belief is absolutely right but it is inadequate by itself. Intellectual assent is not saving trust. Faith is far more than holding a few ideas with your head. It is trusting Christ personally with your whole life, giving yourself to Him, receiving His mighty Holy Spirit, living a new life because you have been made through the Lord's grace.

There is, however, another lesson from what James is trying to teach in this passage. It is linked to works that are done in the name of a false faith, even a demonic one. In the same time that the devil and his demons show orthodoxy in believing in God, they cannot show a genuine faith because they have not been (and will not be) saved by the precious blood of Jesus Christ. We are here reminded that there is also the other side of the coin when we meet many who do great deeds and are completely void of salvation.

Spiritism is a religious sect found in Brazil. It is a spiritualist cult that was developed in France and brought to Brazil with a wide range of acceptance. Its founder, Alain Kardec produced a version of the New Testament—*The Gospel According to Alain Kardec*— which has become the sect's "biblical basis" for their practice. Spiritism is highly involved in doing good deeds; in fact, they are probably the ones doing more for mental health care in the country today. Not only that, their youth are mostly pursuing medical studies for that very reason, to provide medical and mental health care to the poor. It really embarrasses the Christian community in Brazil; both Roman Catholic and Evangelical. They are in hospitals, mental institutions, hospices and other health care programs with a nationwide agenda. Their basic message is that we are saved by good works only. They have faith in God but they do not call themselves to be following any religion. Most of them are Roman Catholics, which is the case in most Latin American countries due to the high level of syncretism that is allowed in that branch of Christendom. The problem is that they evoke the spirits of the dead, they "heal" people through the instrumentality of those spiritual entities. They have weekly sessions where people go in order to either communicate with their beloved ones who have died or to receive *passes* (a form of blessing) for their brokenness, such as love issues, illnesses, and the kind. It is called either "high Spiritism" or "White Spiritism." They call it "white" because their aim is to do good and also they only use white table clothes in their sessions. Their "white" form of religion is opposite to some other forms of Spiritism that use a "darker" form of religion, close to what we may call "Black Magic."

I know of a brother in Christ, "Cássio," who used to be an active member of a *Centro Espírita* (Spiritualist Center—the place where the Kardecist Spiritualists have their sessions) until one day, like the testimony of Saint Augustine, he found a piece of the Scripture in front of him as he was walking home one day. He did not understand what that writing was about, but he knew it was from the Bible. He had a Christian neighbor and went to see him and to inquire what that piece of paper was about. The neighbor, who was praying for him for a long time, told him that he should apply what was there written next time he went to the Centro. It was a portion of 1 John 4 where the Apostle tells his readers to test every spirit to see if it comes from God or not. Cássio went to the Centro that very evening and asked the spirit what the neighbor had given him as a question. This was the basic dialogue Cássio had with the spiritual entity: "Spirit, do you believe there is a God?" The spirit answered, "yes." The next question went like this, "Spirit, do you believe that Jesus Christ came to destroy the works of Satan and to save a people for himself?" At that moment, the demon threw the medium about twenty-five feet from the white clothed table, and, after an agonizing moment left the medium. That was the moment of truth for Cássio, who left the spiritualist center and surrendered his life to Jesus Christ.

James wants to see in his readers the evidence of their faith, "You have faith and I have works. Show me your faith apart from your works, and I will show you my faith by my works." The challenge at this point is crucial for us to realize that our confession of faith must be demonstrated by what we do. This is also related to another example that he brings to us, the one of the tree and its fruits. A dead faith, or a faith without deeds, is like a tree that cannot be seen. It only presupposes that its roots exist, but there is no evidence of a trunk, there are no branches, no leaves are seen. A faith that has fruits is the one that has its roots, but also all of it can be seen, including the fruits. The deeds of faith are the fruits that the tree bears; not only charity, but also fruits of repentance, of justice, and of the Holy Spirit. We read in Matthew 3:8-9, "Produce fruit in keeping with repentance. And do not think you can say to yourselves, 'We have Abraham as our father.' I tell you that out of these stones God can raise up children for Abraham." And Paul writes to the Galatians about the fruit of the Holy Spirit, "But the fruit of the Spirit is love, joy, peace, patience, kindness, goodness, faithfulness, gentleness and self-control" (Galatians 5:22-23).

The Genuine Faith

Genuine faith is better understood as being complete justification. James brings forth two positive illustrations for a better understanding of what a genuine faith really is. By doing this, he is making a direct confrontation with useless faith. It is all related to the basic principle of being born of the Spirit, being made a new creature in Christ Jesus. Simply put, only those who are born of God can have genuine faith. The question still persists, however: How do we know who is a true believer? On the one hand, we are not in God's place to know that, because he is the only one who knows who the elect are. On the other hand, however, the only way for us to know it is through the deeds that our faith will produce.

The Wisdom Of James

The pressing point now is to ascertain if there is any contradiction between what Paul writes in Romans and James in this letter. Are we not justified by faith alone? Yes! We are all justified by faith alone; there is no doubt about that! But to comprehend the two positions, we need to understand the purpose of both letters. The Letter to the Romans was written with an upward, vertical relation to God in mind; the Epistle of James was written from a "down to earth" perspective; that is, with a horizontal direction, related to us believers. For that matter, we should take a moment to see what each of these apostles had to say about being justified by faith and, in James' case, by works.

Paul always affirmed that nobody can be justified by works. A few passages will shed light on this truth. He is emphatic in saying that, "[For] by works of the law no human being will be justified in his sight, since through the law come knowledge of sin" (Romans 3:20). Later on, he states again that, "[For] we hold that one is justified by faith apart from works of the law" (Romans 3:28). Then, as we saw above, he wrote to the Church in Ephesus, "[For] it is by grace you have been saved, through faith—and this not from yourselves, it is the gift of God—not by works, so that no one can boast." Paul is quick, however, to add that we were created for good works, "For we are God's workmanship, created in Christ Jesus to do good works, which God prepared in advance for us to do" (Ephesians 2:10). I understand that Paul deals with the Law in a judicial way, as a procedure for acquittal of humans who are found guilty before the Judgment Seat of the Lord. It embraces more than just doing good deeds, it has to do with the entire aspect of the Law, both the theological and the practical ones. This has to do with our inability to provide the full payment for the total debt we owe to the Lord for being sinners. Of course, this refers to good deeds too. But what I am trying to say is that the predominant aspect of Paul's concern is related to our situation before our Salvation, not after. That is made clear in his entire body of theology; and there is no argument against it. There is absolutely no possibility of salvation apart from faith; any attempt to pursue our defense before God by using whatever religious, philosophical, praxiological arguments we may have will fail. It is by God's complete grace that we are saved, and this

100

The Wisdom Of James

is through faith only. Paul is talking about justification before the Lord, which is between the believer and God himself. Unless one believes in Jesus Christ and his sacrifice on the cross, she will not be justified and nor will he inherit eternal life.

James, on the other hand, writes that "you see that a person is justified by what he does and not by faith alone." What does he really mean by that? Does he mean that we are saved by our works? It seems clear that James is "adding" something else to our "faith alone" orthodoxy. If this is not biblical, we must not follow. If this is not orthodox, we must declare it anathema, and follow Luther's conclusion on the matter. But, James is doing more for our faith than we can imagine; he is liberating us to fulfill the Great Commandment, the Law of Christ, the Royal Law. James is talking about justification after someone believes. We are not saved by works, but saved to do the good works, that is what James is talking about.

Both Paul and James agree that a person is justified by faith. Both use the same illustration for that argument: Abraham. In Romans 4:3 we read, "What does the Scripture say? 'Abraham believed God, and it was credited to him as righteousness.'" James 2:23 says exactly the same thing, "And the Scripture was fulfilled that says, 'Abraham believed God, and it was credited to him as righteousness.'" What we find in James' theology is the reasoning of the evidence of that faith, or righteousness, in a visible way. That is why he argues, "Was not our ancestor Abraham considered righteous for what he did when he offered his son Isaac on the altar?" (v. 21). This is the crux of his argument! He wants the reader to realize that, although Abraham was declared righteous before God entirely by faith; that same faith was demonstrated to us through his action of obedience. One way to put it is this: Faith is the justification cause because Abraham believed first, as we can verify in Genesis 15:6; and Deeds are the result of justification, for Abraham's faith was demonstrated when he obeyed God by taking his only son Isaac and offering him at the altar. That was the moment that God confirmed his faith in him: "Now I know that you fear God, because you have not withheld from me your son, your only son" (Genesis 22:12).

This reminds me of the story of a poor evangelist in Northeast Brazil. He was illiterate and always had someone to read the Bible for him; then, he would memorize the text and go to the villages preaching the Gospel to others. "Joaquim" had a son in elementary school, "Severino." They lived in a place that was very hostile to the Gospel, mostly to the Evangelicals. One day, Severino came home with a question that his teacher asked him in school. He put the question to his father, looking for help. "*Painho* (Daddy), the teacher told me to ask you this, 'If God knew that Abraham believed in him, why did he command Abraham to kill Isaac?'" Joaquim took that whole afternoon to pray about it and come up with an answer. Next morning, Severino went back to school with this answer, "*Tia* (Aunty—the way children call their teachers in grade school), Painho told me this, 'How would I have known of Abraham's faith shouldn't God had commanded him to sacrifice Isaac? And how would I know of his faith if he hadn't obeyed Him?'" This seems to be a very simple illustration, but I believe it has a tremendous application for our lives even today. How would we have known of Abraham's faith if we did not have Genesis 22?

Faith Vindicated Before the World

A very important equation is here proposed: Faith (Genesis 15:6) plus Deeds (Genesis 22:12) equals friendship with God (Isaiah 41:8). This friendship is to be nourished throughout the believers lifetime. There is, however, a further apparent problem in this text that we need to address, as we come to a conclusion for James' argument: What is the real meaning of "justified" in verse 24? We need to explore the word in other contexts in order to clarify what is in James' mind.

The first meaning is *to acknowledge*. It is the recognition of someone, the justification of someone's actions. In fact, it is more than the superficial idea, it is the deeper conviction that it is justified because of a key source of authority. One example that we have is the acknowledgement that God is just, in the NIV translation "that God's way was right," after the people saw what Jesus was doing. The text reads, "(All the people, even the tax collectors, when they heard Jesus' words, acknowledged [justified] that God's way was right, because they had been baptized by John. But the Pharisees and experts in the law rejected God's purpose for themselves, because they had not been baptized by John.)" (Luke 7:29-30). The depth of the meaning is that only those who had been baptized by John were able to "declare God just" (ESV). It is the RSV, however, that makes a more accurate translation of the verb *dikaiou*, "When they heard this all the people and the tax collectors justified God." Luke also uses the same verb with another meaning, *to prove right*, as we can verify, "But wisdom is proved right by all her children" (Luke 7:35, NIV). It has the same weight of the first as we can verify, "Yet wisdom is justified by all her children" (ESV, NKJV, RSV). A third meaning is *to be vindicated*. The previous verse in Luke is translated this way in the NASB version. But there is another that brings forth the same meaning in Paul's writing, "He appeared in a body, was vindicated (justified) by the Spirit, was seen by angels, was preached among the nations, was believed on in the world, was taken up in glory" (1 Timothy 3:16, ESV, NIV, RSV).

In view of those several meanings, which show that the verb *to justify* is being used to provide evidence to other human beings, we may concur with the idea that James is here talking about the Christian being justified; that is, being vindicated before the world through what they do. A person will be justified before God by faith and by demonstrating his or her faith by works. In this way, both God and us will know that one's faith is genuine. Justification by works is the *witness that we are called to bear* wherever we are, whenever we are called to do so. I would like to suggest a tentative paraphrase for verse 24: *You see that a person is justified before God and vindicated as a Christian before men by what he does and not by faith alone.*

James concludes this part with yet another uncommon example: Rahab. She was a woman who was a believer and the only way she demonstrated it in the entire biblical corpus was by lodging the two spies in her house in Jericho. This is the only way we really know that she was a righteous person before the Lord!

We may not completely understand what Justification means in its entirety, but we know that it is a gift from God. When we believe in Jesus Christ as our Savior and Lord, God credits righteousness to us. It is the same idea of a safe box we may have in a bank, we have

The Wisdom Of James

access to it whenever we need. With salvation, when we are justified by our faith, this is credited to us as righteousness, and we have complete access to that credit. But we are called to demonstrate that we have that credit with God through our deeds.

The world is eager to see the good works that come from the People of God. We live an a time that, more than any other, the Church is in great need to show that there is evidence of redemption in Christ Jesus. This is the test of our orthodoxy. Not just words, but they must be evidenced by what we do. It is not a mere ethical thing, it is a whole new paradigm shift, a complete change in our lifestyle, in our worldview. We must walk the talk. John Wesley left a beautiful piece of encouragement for us to consider,

Do all the good you can,
By all the means you can,
In all the ways you can,
In all the places you can,
At all the times you can,
To all the people you can,
As long as ever you can.

Nobody in this earth has been justified by deeds alone. Neither by faith only, because the saving faith will produce good works as a natural result. Faith without deeds is dead and useless. James finalizes the test of our orthodoxy by saying that "the body without spirit is dead, so faith without deeds is dead" (v. 26), and I would like to say that the main characteristics of a dead body is the absence of physical activity and consequent corruption. A believer who does not exercise his or her faith through good works is the same thing: dead and decomposing. May the Lord have mercy on us and restore our Christian lives to the stature of his Son Jesus Christ.

Chapter 9

The Use of the Tongue: The Test of Maturity

James 3:1-12

When I was about ten years old, I made a mistake that I will never forget: There was going to be a surprise birthday party for our Pastor's wife, and I "innocently" told her about it. My tongue betrayed me and that was really an embarrassing situation not only for me, but for my parents as well. I remember how my mother felt about it; she could not find enough words to apologize to all in my behalf. Of course everybody had a good time, and I made history in my home church. Not long ago, a prominent figure in American politics, not aware his microphone was still on, made a rather unwise comment on a Black presidential candidate. It was a national embarrassment for that person who claims to be a Baptist minister as well. The problem was not the microphone but his tongue; he should not have used it to say what he said in the first place.

It is said that a normal man will say approximately 25,000 words a day, while a normal woman will say 30,000. The statistics would help us with some interesting figures: We spend one fifth of our lives talking; we would easily fill a fifty page book a day; and we would fill 132 books of 400 pages in just one year.

The text for this chapter starts by talking about those who want to be teachers; or, as James puts it, "not many of you should presume

The Wisdom Of James

to be teachers, my brothers, because you know that we who teach will be judged more strictly." It humbles me, because I see that our brother James is talking to me in a very special way. Here, he also continues his approach to the issue of wisdom, which will be the topic for the next chapter.

More than anything, however, this passage deals with yet another test: the test of our maturity as Christians. If we know how to handle our tongues, we are mature Christians and this will show to the world around us that we are different because of our faith. In dealing with the issue of wisdom, I perhaps should say, this passage deals with false wisdom, which is shown by the unwise use of the tongue. Now, we need to link this important teaching to our daily walk as members of the Kingdom of God, the kingdom from above. We must be aware of this teaching as a test of our own maturity as Christians; the world is often checking us out. But above all, we have the privilege of being ready to demonstrate to the world that the Lord is the one who will help us to tame our tongue.

Be Humble! All of Us Fail in this Matter

As pointed above, James addresses the issue of teaching, "Not many of you should presume to be teachers." It is not a discouragement for someone who wants to become a teacher in the church; rather, it is an admonition to be conscious of the fact that teaching is a rather difficult task and will require a greater amount of commitment. There is the danger of pride, some tendency of becoming the "Rabbi"—"My great one!" This source of pride is demonic and should not be tolerated in the church, or anywhere else.

It is sad to see how much damage a proud teacher brings to a church. So many illustrations surface at this point, but it is not the time to point fingers at anyone. We must attain to the core of James teaching at this point. We see, however, that he is in line with all those Bible authors who, inspired by the Holy Spirit, talk about the false teachers. They are devastating and no one today will skip their fangs. A quick admonition from Paul will help us at this point. When writing to his disciple Timothy, he makes sure that in the last days those false teachers would be around (1 Timothy 4:1-3). It is impor-

106

The Wisdom Of James

tant to note that those teachers are filled with demons, and because of that, they keep deceiving others. He continues his teaching by describing the false teachers in his second letter to Timothy (2 Timothy 3:1-9). The sad news is that the people in the Church will also be ready to receive their teaching. As Paul points out, "the time will come when men will not put up with sound doctrine. Instead, to suit their own desires, they will gather around them a great number of teachers to say what their itching ears want to hear. They will turn their ears away from the truth and turn aside to myths" (2 Timothy 4:3-4).

James helps us realize that the use of our tongue will serve as a gauge to measure our Christian maturity in several ways. The tongue will preserve life and happiness, according to the Apostle Peter, "Whoever would love life and see good days must keep his tongue from evil and his lips from deceitful speech" (1 Peter 3:10). It also teaches us not to judge others, "Do not judge, or you too will be judged. For in the same way you judge others, you will be judged, and with the measure you use, it will be measured to you" (Matthew 7:1-2). In this particular case, the danger is set around idle conversation, gossip, and premature judgment of others. Many of us are aware of this dreadful situation; how many marriages have been broken because of gossip! How many lives have been literarily destroyed because of some small talk that became as big as the fire of Chicago! Although we are instructed by Paul that we should check if we find ourselves in Christ (2 Corinthians 13:5), only Jesus Christ knows what is going on in someone's life. There is also a place for judgment in the Church, this is expected to be done in love and with the desire to help the person in fault to return from his or her sin—I am talking about Church discipline here (cf. Matthew 18:15-20). What the Bible teaches against in Matthew 7, however, is to judge someone without first making a self evaluation in order to point the error in the other person.

I believe that James is trying to tell us how humble everyone of us must be when we face the sad reality of the misuse of our tongue. He points out that, "We all stumble in many ways." Here we find him including himself among the readers of the Epistle. He knows quite well that "no man can tame the tongue." And this includes him as well. Paul also includes himself among sinners, as we will find in his letter to Timothy, "Here is a trustworthy saying that deserves full acceptance: Christ Jesus came into the world to save sinners— of whom I am the worst" (1 Timothy 1:15). All of us stumble in some areas of our lives: our affections, our will, our minds, and so on, are some of those areas where we stumble the most. But James takes one example that is common to all of us, without exception: THE TONGUE! In order to make this point clearer, he says, "If anyone is never at fault in what he says, he is a perfect man, able to keep his whole body in check" (v. 2). Of course, this remark from James applies only to Jesus Christ. He is the perfect one who never committed sin.

Not long ago, a brother of a member of one of the churches I served as a pastor refused to stay for his funeral because he did not agree with me theologically. I learned about that through someone else during the fellowship meal we shared together after the funeral. For my surprise, I had never met that gentleman before; he lived in another state and I briefly saw him at the hospital the day his brother passed away. His judgment was totally based on his own assumptions about my faith and because I was not from his ethnic-oriented expression of Christianity. My response to that bit of information was, "And he didn't even talk with me to find out how much we might agree theologically." Sometimes our surface perceptions about others lead us to betray our tongue; it is key to make sure what we see and act upon it. Only eternity will disclose the intents of many a heart.

How many times do the ghosts of our past haunt us for things we have spoken that cannot be corrected? I was sitting in church before my time to preach when we had the children's sermon for that particular Sunday morning. One of our valuable Sunday school teachers gathered the children up front and started to teach them by using a toothpaste tube. There was I just trying to figure out what was the practical or objective lesson for the morning. She asked one of the children to squeeze the tube and we saw a lot of toothpaste come out of it. Then, the teacher asked that child to put the paste back into the tube. That was impossible to happen at that time. Only then we all understood the objective lesson: Like our words out of our mouths, that paste, once out of the tube, could not return into it. What a simple way of putting it before us! (We sometimes learn more from children sermons than we even expect.) There are instances in our lives that we deeply regret and many of them are related to words that we have spoken to hurt others.

This is one area that all of us have a problem with. There is no escape; we are guilty as charged. Therefore, we should be humble and agree with the brother of Jesus Christ who knew that there was only one Person who could not be charged with that sin, our Lord Jesus Christ, the Perfect man. It is comforting to learn this because such a humbling situation puts us as equals before the throne of God. In that case, all of us are standing before him with the same need. As James included himself among his brothers and sisters, so do I.

Learning How to Tame Our Tongue

The main point that James wants to make is that of self-control, which is one of the fruits of the Spirit. To illustrate this, he draws six different examples related to self-discipline. For him, to tame the tongue is a very key element of Christian conduct. Unless we are able to tame it, we will not live lives that demonstrate God's love in our hearts. The six examples are taken from horses, ships, forests, animals, springs of water, and trees.

The Discipline of Our Body

The first example is the horse. The control of power, of strength. The horse is one of the most intelligent animals on earth, yet it does not know anything about its strength. It is necessary that a person use bits to keep it under control. The same idea applies to our tongue: it can destroy our body if not tamed.

The other example is the ship, which deals with the control of our ways, of our paths. Although a ship is so big, her rudder is a tiny piece of equipment. The captain will lead her wherever he wants her to go. The same should be said about our tongue: a small organ of our body which will lead us to many places. It would lead us to success in life, but also to complete destruction.

The Discipline of Our Influence Upon Others

Here we are dealing with our sphere of influence. Being a teacher, or making disciples through our testimonies, we need to keep in mind that we will influence the lives of many people. In my own experience, one of the men who most influenced my life was my father and the way he handles his tongue. He is a man of few words but he has tremendously spoken to me through his actions. I know of many who have come to Jesus through his ministry, and most of them never heard him preach to them; my Dad simply does not preach. His message of the Gospel of Jesus is conveyed through the way he conducts himself and his life.

Fire is a constant danger because it spreads easily and with a tremendous rage. Just as an illustration, allow me to refer to the Chicago fire that happened in 1871: "On October 8, 1871, at about 8:30 p.m. history tells us that Mrs. O'Leary's cow kicked over a lantern and started the most destructive fire in the history of our country. The great Chicago fire destroyed 17,500 buildings, left 300 dead, 100,000 homeless, and cost 400 million dollars." Someone once said that the tongue is "dynamite in your dentures." I think it is related to anything one say to the others that will hurt them. Perhaps the main source of fire through the tongue comes from gossip.

Gossip spreads very quickly. It will hurt a great number of people. Maybe many of us today are hurt and the source of it would probably come from gossip. It is said that someone who gossips to you will certainly gossip about you. The tongue is said to have power of death and life. "The tongue has the power of life and death, and those who love it will eat its fruit" (Proverbs 18:21). I know of a pastor who was literally precluded of doing his ministry in his homeland because a gossip about him. Only after eighteen years did that pastor realize what was going on. As he pursued the source of the gossip, which was not entirely disclosed, he realized that the "spark of fire" was completely unfounded but then it was too late to try to repair any damage behind it.

Another illustration is taken from Adolf Hitler. He wrote the book *Mein Kamft* and it is said that for each word of that book, 125 lives were lost in World War II. It seems strange to use this illustration, not of spoken works, but written ones; I venture to say that most of the works in that book were spoken by Hitler in his speeches all over Germany in those days.

The Discipline of Our Own Nature

James took examples from nature to show us that we should also tame our own nature. He introduces different animals, "animals, birds, reptiles and creatures of the sea are being tamed and have been tamed by man, *but no man can tame the tongue. It is a restless evil, full of deadly poison*" (vv. 7-8, emphasis added). This talks about our problems with hatred, evil talking, and the like. It has to do with our temper and the way we relate to each other. The other example that he draws from nature is the spring of water. It has to do with the ambiguity of our talk in many ways. The text says that the same tongue that praises the Lord curses other persons, who are made in God's likeness. A poet, unknown to me, once put this perspective in the following way:

> *A careless word may kindle strife.*
> *A cruel word may wreck a life.*
> *A bitter word may hate instill.*
> *A brutal word may smite and kill.*
>
> *A gracious word may smooth the way.*
> *A joyous word may light the day.*
> *A timely word may lessen stress.*
> *A loving word may heal and bless.*

James also talks about the tree and its fruits. Again, we will know the tree by its fruits. It is told that a young Christian man got angry on the job and lost his temper. He said oaths and curses and then he was so embarrassed and tried to give an explanation: "I don't know why I said that. It really isn't me." The other partner wisely replied: "It had to be in you or it couldn't have come out of you." This has to do with our human nature: we are fallen people and we desperately need God to solve our problems.

I wish to be like Jesus,
So humble and so kind
His words were always tender,
His voice was e'ver divine.

But no, I'm not like Jesus,
As everyone can see!
O Savior, come and help me,
And make me just like Thee.
(Anonymous)

"My brothers, this should not be." The consequences of what we say will be found here and in eternity. "But I tell you that men will have to give account on the day of judgment for every careless word they have spoken" (Matthew 12:36).

We cannot help ourselves: "No man can tame the tongue." Only through the help of God himself, through his Holy Spirit, will we be able to tame our tongue. With the Psalmist, we should pray daily, "Set a guard over my mouth, O LORD; keep watch over the door of my lips" (Psalm 141:3). Also, with the Preacher, we should say, "Pleasant words are a honeycomb sweet to the soul and healing to the bones" (Proverbs 16:24). As we sing a new song everyday, let us come before the Lord and sing, "May the words of my mouth and the meditation of my heart be pleasing in your sight, O LORD, my Rock and my Redeemer" (Psalm 19:14).

The Tongue and the Call to Teach

It is important that we go back to the initial admonition that James has for those who want to be or presume to be teachers. This is a most important piece of advice that we may find in Scripture for us. I include myself in this group because I have a proven ministry as both a pastor and a teacher. It is a very difficult task in Christian ministry because we, teachers, are in the "business" of modeling people for life and also for ministry. Anything we do and say through our teaching will shape the next generation. It humbles me to learn that a former student of mine is doing ministry in a different part of the world and that he is using what I have conveyed to him in classroom. The question often comes to my mind (and my heart): Did I teach what was the right thing? Only through the results of their ministry will I know what I did right or wrong.

In the same line of concern, it is necessary to point once again that James wants to make sure that his readers will attain a level of maturity that supercedes the requirements of the world. If on the one hand we may find people who make vows of silence in order to not fall in the traps of the tongue; on the other hand we should realize that the other extreme is not to become versed in any kind of new rhetoric. The foundation of a faith that is mature is to have control of the tongue. This applies to every Christian; but now I want to emphasize that James seems to be dealing with the issue of people who were presuming to be teacher without the level of maturity that they were expected to have.

In many ways, it is very difficult to gauge what we teach but we should be humble enough to allow the Spirit of God to work in our lives in order to help us improve, correct some mistakes, and so forth. Above all, we should allow the Spirit lead us in the Word to grant us the wisdom that we need as teachers. I believe this is what James wanted to convey to those who were teaching among the members of the Christian Church spread around the world. This is the topic of our next chapter.

Chapter 10

Two Kinds of Wisdom: Handling Them Wisely

James 3:13-18

On a personal level, the issue of future decisions is a constant concern for most of us. We now proceed to one of the most important aspects of James' teaching: the way we handle wisdom. Here we may suggest that even the most cliché question is again the key inquiry into what God wants for our lives: "What is God's will for my life?" This question came to me from friend of mine one evening. It sounds too simplistic but at the same time, this is one of the most important questions one should ask. This is a question we all ask on a regular basis: when we have major decisions to make, when a new career becomes an inviting option, or when someone shows up in one's life as a potential husband or wife. That was my friend's case. It amazes me how many are those who fail in making their decisions as they choose their wives or husbands! Don't get me wrong, I am not talking about this particular friend of mine. He later made a very wise decision and is happily married today. But one thing is important to point out here: we need God's wisdom to know God's will.

This chapter started to take shape when we were talking about asking God for wisdom. In order to know God's will, we certainly need to learn God's wisdom. But I have noticed that wherever I go,

The Wisdom Of James

be it in the United States or abroad, the wisdom of God has been a matter of great questioning. What I want to add is that there has been a flood of false prophets and false teachers invading Christendom with a fierce impact. This leads me to Paul with his several admonitions about the end of the days, when demonic forces (i.e., deceiving spirits) would increase their dominance over the members of Jesus Christ's Church; many of those following the teaching that will be in line with their own lusts and spiritual desires. It is worth quoting him at this point, "Now the Spirit expressly says that in later times some will depart from the faith by devoting themselves to deceitful spirits and teachings of demons, through the insincerity of liars whose consciences are seared. . . . Just as Jannes and Jambres opposed Moses, so these men also oppose the truth, men corrupted in mind and disqualified regarding the faith. But they will not get very far, for their folly will be plain to all, as was that of those two men" (1 Timothy 4:1-2; 2 Timothy 3:8-9). The whole issue of wisdom in the Church has everything to do with the need for us to come to the Lord and learn from him how to discern the difference between what is from above and what is from below.

We read in Chapter 1:5 that, "If any of you lacks wisdom, he should ask God, who gives generously to all without finding fault, and it will be given to him." Now we have another test before us; one that James has divided in two parts in Chapter 3. The first part deals with the test of maturity, and now we will deal with the test of handling wisdom properly.

Wisdom is a difficult thing to acquire. Many of us have a problem in differentiating wisdom from knowledge. As stated before, there are many knowledgeable people who lack a tremendous amount of wisdom. In fact, wisdom is how to apply knowledge or the lack of it properly. I have found very wise men and women amongst the illiterate people in villages around the world. I have also found very foolish men and women amongst the superbly literate people in sophisticated metropolitans areas, not only in my homeland, but also in North America and in Europe. This is a matter of most serious investigation for our daily lives; there are those who live their lives in total lack of wisdom, sucking the breath and breadth from those who have them.

Again, James is bringing forth the main subject of his Epistle: "Let faith be proved by deeds, let wisdom be shown by works." This text explains more clearly the difference between false and true wisdom. The former is not from heaven, the latter is from God, "from above." James is still dealing with self-appointed teachers, those he mentioned in the beginning of the third chapter. There he starts to address this topic by pointing to the instrument of their failure: their tongue. For them, the tongue is the instrument of false wisdom; therefore, he asks, "who is wise and understanding among you?" False wisdom is shown through pride, disputes, bitterness, and an eagerness to defeat their opponents, instead of establishing the truth. Then James moves from false wisdom towards what true wisdom really is. He knows that false wisdom leads to death, but that "there is heavenly wisdom for earthly living."

It is my desire in this chapter to address the biblical basis for handling wisdom. Obviously I am not alone when I say that I need this study applied to my own life in the first place; I lack wisdom in many areas of my life and I hope the Lord will continue to administer his Word in me in such a way that I will be fortunate enough not to commit so many mistakes in the years to come. It is proper to say that we all lack wisdom; only God has it in abundance to dispense through his grace upon us. As we deal with this topic, yet another test is put before us: the test of handling wisdom properly.

We Need to Learn About the Origin of Wisdom

James uses a series of parallelisms in this passage; he tries to show three basic things about both types of wisdom: their origin, their function, and their results. As we explore their origin, we will find out that they come from totally opposite directions. False wisdom comes from below; true wisdom comes from above.

False Wisdom "does not come down from heaven but is earthly, unspiritual, of the devil" (v. 15). James uses a very easy to understand way to describe the sources of both wisdoms. Here he uses the imagery that people will grasp and he starts with the concept from below. His dramatic description does not concede any chance for a middle ground concept. There is no compromising wisdom:

either it is from above or from below. In dealing with false wisdom, he presents three qualifiers that do not show any possibility of misunderstanding.

It is Earthly. It means that it has its roots not in Heaven, not in God. It depends upon earthly knowledge and "propaganda." It is generated basically by worldly desires that appeal to us. It is completely contrary to God's Word. A similar contrast between the two wisdoms is also depicted by Paul to the Corinthians when he compares the wisdom of the world against the wisdom of God, that is the Gospel of the Kingdom (1 Corinthians 1-2). It is the kind of wisdom that also has affected theology in many ways. It is understood that we have two kinds of theologizing: one from above and another from below. The former is directed by the revelation of God and the former is somewhat idealized by whoever is doing the theologizing. This invites further scrutiny, beyond the scope of this study. When I bring forth this distinction, as a missiologist and also as a theologian, I need to be reminded that it is the wisdom from above that illuminates whatever perception I have of the spiritual reality, which in most cases come from my own view, from my own investigation. There is nothing wrong in having a theology from below, as long as we submit it to the revealed truth from above (2 Corinthians 10:4-5). But I have reason to believe that James was going much further than what is the methodological way of doing theology; he is concerned with the center of Theology itself: the Wisdom of God as revealed to us. In dealing with the entire chapter; we are to be reminded that he is dealing with those who want to be teachers. Therefore, I see that this point will help the teacher to know where he or she is in the theologizing process as well.

It is Unspiritual. This is also translated as "sensual" (NKJV). It has nothing to do with the new life that Christ offers through the Holy Spirit. "The man without the Spirit does not accept the things that come from the Spirit of God, for they are foolishness to him, and he cannot understand them, because they are spiritually discerned" (1 Corinthians 2:14). Back to the false teachers, how could they make a clear and sound declaration of God's purpose if they do not grasp the spiritual reality? The same with common members of the church who are not able to discern the spiritual things. We live in a world that is rather sensual; focused on its own hedonism. We live in a world that, as Harold Brown calls it in his book, is immersed in "The Sensate Culture." The literature that describes our world today is vast and intriguing in many aspects. The most radical changes in our "un-spirituality" started when the world's self definition shifted from above to below, with its culmination in the Enlightenment. These past fifty years, however, have been the portrait of the collapse of our human wisdom; it is better described by the postmodern agenda that is already spread and present in all parts of the world.

It is of the Devil. The reason for such a strong statement from James is the fact that the devil is the father of all lies, and any kind of "wisdom" that does not come out of truth comes from his mouth. Jesus told the Jews that even though they called themselves children of Abraham (by tradition), they were children of the devil: "You belong to your father, the devil, and you want to carry out your father's desire. He was a murderer from the beginning, not holding to the truth, for there is no truth in him. When he lies, he speaks his native language, for he is a liar and the father of lies" (John 8:44). Here James closes the circle of the three elements that lead the believer to walk outside the will of God: the world, the flesh and the devil. The wisdom from below (i.e., from the world) is closely related to the wisdom of the flesh, which in itself is manipulated by the devil. We may see here the correlation with a Satanic form of religion as well. The wisdom that does not come from the Lord is in itself used by the devil to manipulate the minds and will of those who are not in Christ.

True Wisdom comes from God Himself, "but the wisdom that comes from heaven" (v. 17). Opposing to the mundane, unspiritual and devilish wisdom, True Wisdom has a divine source. It comes from heaven, from above. This is the wisdom that transforms the hearts and the minds of those who receive the new birth, those who are born of the Spirit (Cf. John 3:3, 5; Ephesians 2:5). The natural person cannot understand this wisdom unless the Holy Spirit gives him or her the power to grasp the mysteries of God, as Paul says, "[it is] spiritually discerned" (1 Corinthians 2:14b). It is impossible for a natural person understand the plan of salvation; it is impossible for a natural person to understand the holiness of God, it is simply impossible for them to discern what only the Holy Spirit can show to them. People may have a grasp of what moral laws are alike because the Lord has given human race a level of consciousness that will resemble part of his natural laws. Two quick arguments in this direction: first, common grace allows for the reflection of God's image in people, even though the human race has broken that image through sin. Secondly, our conscience becomes in itself our own law before the Lord and before other human beings. Before God, it will be used in the Day of the Lord, before human beings, there are many codes of law that reflect some level of justice, even though those who wrote them have no knowledge of the Living God. But the True Wisdom is meta-cosmic, it is revealed by the Lord. That is why James affirms that it comes from heaven.

True wisdom is acclaimed all over the Bible, but the best place to learn its importance is found in the book of Proverbs. The purpose of that book is stated in its very beginning: "for attaining wisdom and discipline, for understanding words of insight" (Proverbs 1:2). Also, "Blessed is the man who finds wisdom, the man who gains understanding, for she is more profitable than silver and yields better returns than gold. She is more precious than rubies; nothing you desire can compare with her" (Proverbs 3:13-15).

True wisdom is the perfect gift from God: "Every good and perfect gift is from above, coming down from the Father of the heavenly lights, who does not change like shifting shadows" (James 1:17). True wisdom is the most precious gift in the Person of Jesus Christ (Proverbs 8:22-31), the Only Begotten Son of God (John 3:16). Because of this, True Wisdom is the Gospel that has power to transform our lives (Romans 1:16-17; 1 Corinthians 1-2).

We Need to Learn How It Operates

False wisdom operates in accordance to its earthly, unspiritual and devilish roots. Using this concept in a crescendo, we will realize that it works in four ways: Jealousy, selfish ambition, boasting and deceit.

The Bible tells us that we have many ways to pursue life: "there is a way that seems right to a man, but in the end it leads to death"

The Wisdom Of James

(Proverbs 14:12). We are invited to always check our priorities in life. There are many who go through life regretting the unwise decisions they have made over the years. This is understandable because some bad decisions will leave marks and wounds that will take a long time to dissipate in the air. Only God's forgiveness will help erase the memories of decisions that have caused so much pain to self or to others. James is here, as he does consistently in his epistle, showing the practical effects of wisdom. In the first place, he shows the negative results of false wisdom. It has everything to do with people's selfishness and their inability of looking beyond themselves. This is how he puts it: "But if you harbor bitter envy and selfish ambition in your hearts, do not boast about it or deny the truth" (v. 14).

The problem with bitterness and envy is deeply related with the breaking of the Tenth Commandment, "You shall not covet your neighbor's house." It is an inward sin against God and our neighbor. Paul dealt with this issue when he was struggling with the fight between what the law leads us to see and what we should do as we walk in Jesus. The same he points out in his letter to the Galatians, when he makes the distinction between walking in the Spirit and conceding to the power of the flesh (Cf. Romans 6-8; Galatians 5). A bitter heart and an envious eye are the worst enemies of the believer in Jesus Christ. They are the embodiment of what comes from false wisdom. In some aspect, marketing is a good illustration of this. Among the strong rules of advertising, the hook is geared towards the desire of acquiring what you see out there as the attainable impossibility. It appeals to what you are craving inside, it goes deeply to one's sense of envy and lust.

Many are those who thrive through the fuel of false wisdom. They do not want to mature as human beings, and when their lives are sickened by that wisdom, they live lives that do not honor the Lord. The results are painfully degrading to the Christian testimony among others. James describes it this way, "For where jealousy and selfish ambition exist, there will be disorder and every vile practice" (v. 16).

A word should be said about ambition. There is nothing wrong with the term, for it will help one to reach the many goals he or she has set for their lives. I have met a number of people who tell me that "my ambition is to know God better," for example. There are others who have the ambition of helping others in many ways: as volunteers, as helpers in times of need, as missionaries, and so forth. But when it becomes self-centered, it takes a different turn.

True Wisdom operates in many different ways, but we will deal with those that are closer to the mind of James in this passage: First, *it deals with our attitude*, with our conduct. It leads to a *humble lifestyle*. Humility is one of the key virtues of the wise follower of Jesus Christ. Paul covers this issue in various passages. For a moment, I'd like to use his teaching in Romans (12:3) which teaches us to humbly walk before God and humankind in a soberly way. By knowing who we are in Christ we are able to see who we are before others. Along with that, we are to walk in *purity of life*, we have a holy life, because the Lord is Holy. Then we must have a *peaceful life*, we are the true peacemakers of the world because we serve the Prince of Peace. *Gentleness* or a *considerate life* is also a great demonstration of our wisdom. Sometimes we need to learn how to back off and wait for the Lord to work the situation in his own way. Finally, our attitude will be shown wisely through a *submissive life*. I prefer calling this "open to reason lifestyle." We should be open to receive criticism and be open for change.

Secondly, *it deals with our actions*. We should live *merciful lives*, as the Lord teaches in the Sermon on the Mount, "Blessed are the merciful, for they will be shown mercy" (Matthew 5:7). As we use to say, "put yourself in someone's shoes." Have compassion for those who are in need. James mentions *"good fruit."* This leads us to one of the great writings of Paul, when he addresses our walk in the Spirit. We should bear the fruit of the Spirit (Galatians 5:22-23), but this is just the reason why we have been chosen by the Lord. He chose us to bear fruit, many fruit (John 15:16).

Thirdly, *it deals with our area of judgment*. It should be *impartial and sincere*. This is also linked with walking a life that is full of mercy for others. It is James who reminds us that we should not judge others without mercy, "Speak and act as those who are going to be judged by the law that gives freedom, because judgment

The Wisdom Of James

without mercy will be shown to anyone who has not been merciful. Mercy triumphs over judgment" (2:12-13).

We Need to Learn About Its Results

The results of false wisdom can be seen in this parallel demonstration, as we can see below. Another way of putting it is this: whatever you sow, you end up reaping. This is such a simple teaching! "We are what we eat," say some; so we are what we know. We act in accordance to what we know in most cases; consciously or not, we reflect what kind of wisdom we attain. There is a saying from Jesus that intrigues me, "If then the light in you is darkness, how great is the darkness" (Matthew 6:23b). In that same way, I keep thinking, when I try to paraphrase that same thought: If then the wisdom in you is foolishness, how great is that foolishness. There are so many who are fools who think they are wise. But in the end of the day, their foolishness is so deep that no one can fathom how shallow they really are.

Where you have	There you find
envy	disorder
selfish ambition	every evil practice

The results of true wisdom, on the other end, are described in a most wonderful way: "and the harvest, which righteousness yields to the peacemakers, comes from a sowing of peace" (v. 18). Kistemaker brings the following comment on this important part of the Scripture,

Although we wholeheartedly affirm our desire for peace in the context of family, church, society, and nation, we have reservations when we are told to seek peace at any price. We do not wish to compromise truth, for such a compromise is equivalent to promoting falsehood. We cannot set aside the rules of conduct we derive from Scripture. Thus we stand firm in our defense of our Christian heritage.

Within the context of church and society, however, Christians have often preached the love of God and have quoted verses of Scripture to prove their point, but in practice have shown the least love toward their neighbor. In fact, the liberal in the church or the humanist in society often demonstrates a greater degree of love for his fellow man than does the person who cites chapter and verse from the pages of the Bible. Unfortunately, Christians frequently give the world the impression that they are more interested in strife and confrontation than in peace and love.

How true! So many times have we noticed the heavy judgmental display of unkindness and prejudice in place of wisdom from heaven. Unfortunately the world continues to wait for a truthful attitude that reflects the law of love, which is exercised by the law of liberty (2:12). An attitude that shows mercy that triumphs over judgment (2:13b). The ultimate result of heavenly wisdom is peace by those who make peace (v.18). That peace is the mark of the children of God, for "Blessed are the peacemakers, for they shall be called sons of God" (Matthew 5:9).

As a conclusion to this chapter, let us pray that the Lord will help us make three important decisions in our lives: First, let us go to our knees in prayer: "If any one lacks wisdom, he should ask God, who gives generously to all without finding fault, and it will be given to him" (1:5). Secondly, let us go to the Word of God: "Your commands make me wiser than my enemies, for they are ever with me. I have more insight than all my teachers, for I meditate on your statutes. I have more understanding than the elders, for I obey your precepts" (Psalm 119:98-100). Thirdly, let us go to the Wise: "He who walks with the wise grows wise, but a companion of fools suffers harm" (Proverbs 13:20).

Chapter 11

Asking With the Wrong Motives: The Test of Prayer

James 4:1-3

After learning about the two kinds of wisdom and how to handle them wisely, we come now to an important test that James brings to the fore: how to apply wisdom in our priorities, and mostly, which is the case of this passage, to our prayer life? The fourth chapter of the Epistle has two key teachings related to wisdom; the first is related to prayer, the second with our submission to God's will. In both cases, there is a great need to have a solid and healthy relationship with God. This is the theme that will satisfy both applications of wisdom: through a healthy personal relationship with our Lord we will know what to ask in prayer, but also what to set as priorities in our lives.

During my last year in Seminary, back in Brazil, I received the invitation to serve as a pastor of a small Portuguese-speaking Church in Johannesburg, South Africa. I contacted my Presbytery and they gave me the green flag to accept the invitation and work towards my going to that beautiful city. Since I am Presbyterian, I prayed to the Lord asking from him that the final answer should come from the Presbytery. Although I am personally accountable to Jesus Christ as my Lord, I am also accountable to those who hold authority over me, those who have been instituted as such by the Lord himself through

The Wisdom Of James

his Holy Scripture. The plan was to have me ordained during our January meeting and then be released to go to my new mission field a few weeks later. Accordingly, I had my paperwork already in the South African Embassy in Brasília, my tickets had been reserved and all I had to do was to be ordained.

The weekend of my ordination came soon. I was interviewed by the Presbytery committees on theology and on ordination, and followed all the procedures for it. But I had not heard the final word from the Presbytery yet. It was Saturday afternoon and I was called to yet another committee for an interview. It sounded out of place because I knew everything had been done already and I was to be ordained that Sunday evening. The brothers of the committee told me that some new developments had taken place during the weekend that included me. The two presbyteries in town had decided to form a new seminary to begin offering classes the following month. The problem they were facing was that there was not any professor of Hebrew and Old Testament Studies for the new formed seminary and I was their only candidate. Thus those brothers told me that the Presbytery could not let me go to South Africa. Although they told me that I had the right of refusing their decision, I was expected to comply with that most important need for the seminary. The problem that I had before me was another: since I had been praying that the final answer was to come from the Presbytery, that was the final answer for me. With tears in my eyes, I submitted to their authority and was ordained at the Campinas Presbyterian Church in Goiânia, Brazil, on Sunday January 9, 1983.

As a result of that act of obedience, I became the first professor of Hebrew and Old Testament Studies at the Brasil Central Presbyterian Seminary. As the days went by, I had the privilege of meeting my wife, getting married, moving to the United States, and the rest is just history. When I look back, I see God's hands in everything. The other crucial piece of this puzzle is the fact that I was not prepared to serve in a cross-cultural setting at that time—I now realize. I have reasons to believe that should I have gone to Johannesburg, my mistakes there would have been so many that probably I would be out of the ministry today.

This chapter deals specifically with prayer as the "mandatory" rule to submit to God's will. The test of our faith continues and this time it is the test of our prayerful life. Later in this Epistle, James will touch the issue of prayer again, but the focus then will be different from the one here. Therefore, I will deal with prayer as a test of true wisdom; it comes to us as a negative approach to the issue because James seems to be dealing with the unwise way of praying. In other way of putting it, he seems to capitalize on bad prayer habits as yet another result of lacking in wisdom that comes from above. Nonetheless, prayer is a mandatory rule for us to have the courage to submit ourselves to God's plan for our lives. The continuing arguments in his fourth chapter will make it clear. Later on in his epistle, he comes back to prayer from another angle; so will I in two more chapters that deal with that subject. Right now, our main theme leads us to see the contours of yet another test, the test of prayer.

Lack of Wisdom Brings Forth Fights and Quarrels

Opposite to what James says at the very end of Chapter 3, when he demonstrates that the fruit of wisdom from heaven is peace, now he introduces a question that not only continues his view on false wisdom, but has a deep bearing on our relationship with God, starting with prayer. At the center of his new chapter, he wants to show that wisdom is exercised in personal relationship with the Lord. The question is right to the point, "What causes fights and quarrels among you? Don't they come from your desires that battle within you?" (v. 1).

The cause of fights and quarrels is linked with lack of wisdom, which is found in 3:14 "But if you harbor bitter envy and selfish ambition...", and also in 3:16, "For where you have envy and selfish ambition, there you find disorder and every evil practice." Fights and quarrels (in other versions: War) are related to conflicts within the body of Christ as well as within the Christian person. Phillips translates it in this way, "But what about the feuds and struggles that exist among you—where do you suppose they come from? Can't you see that they arise from conflicting passions within yourselves?"

The Wisdom Of James

Usually those fights and quarrels are the result of *lack of inner peace* in one's heart. It is the result of the conflict between the desires of our flesh and the Spirit who is in us. This somehow reflects well the increasing number of cases of anxiety related disorders in our society. We seem to be unconscious of the deep spiritual roots of anxiety; therefore, we do not treat it as a consequence of our sinful nature. It is just natural for a person who does not know how to walk in the Spirit to succumb to the desperation of lack of wisdom. The result is soon manifested: all sorts of anxiety attacks invade those hearts. We learn in Galatians 5:16-17 that we should live by the Spirit, "and you will not gratify the desires of the sinful nature. For the sinful nature desires what is contrary to the Spirit, and the Spirit what is contrary to the sinful nature. They are in conflict with each other, so that you do not do what you want." The sinful nature shows these acts: "The acts of the sinful nature are obvious: sexual immorality, impurity and debauchery, idolatry and witchcraft; hatred, discord, jealousy, fits of rage, selfish ambition, dissensions, factions and envy; drunkenness, orgies, and the like" (Galatians 5:20).

James Nieboer brings forth a sober description of the several sources of quarrels amongst people. In his view, much can be drawn from Scripture itself as it points to some men who showed their character. "So the real trouble was self-pleasing and self-love. Herod got into trouble because of the love of pleasure (Mark 6:14-29); Judas, because of the love of money (Mark 14:10,11); Hezekiah, because of the love of display (2 Kings 20:12-18); Adoni-bezek, because of the love of power (Judges 1:5-7); and Diotrophes, because of the love of pre-eminence (3 John 9,10)." But again, when we turn back to Jesus, he also spoke about the source of much jealousy and fighting as he taught about what defiles a person: "And he said, 'What comes out of a person is what defiles him. For from within, out of the heart of man, come evil thoughts, sexual immorality, theft, murder, adultery, coveting, wickedness, deceit, sensuality, envy, slander, pride, foolishness. All these evil things come from within, and they defile a person'" (Mark 7:20-23).

Therefore, the purpose of our prayers is to glorify God (1 Corinthians 10:31), not to seek our own favor or pleasure. The secret of a peaceful life is found in our life of prayer. We should

The Wisdom Of James

pray according to the will of God (1 John 5:14; cf. Matthew 26:39). Only then we will experience his gracious and perfect will for our lives. But, in order for this to happen, we must be aware that we first need to be *in Christ*. That is why the Apostle Paul talks about Jesus Christ living in us: "I have been crucified with Christ and I no longer live, but Christ lives in me. The life I live in the body, I live by faith in the Son of God, who loved me and gave himself for me" (Galatians 2:20). This reminds us of the humble attitude that we must have before God: "Not I, but Christ!" The secret of what James wants to convey is the great need of all of us to be filled with the wisdom of God in our hearts and minds. Our positioning of the heart *over* the mind is primarily because our own existence is relational, and that relationship is centered in Jesus Christ as a person. Paul is the theologian who most dealt with this concept of being *in Christ* as the prerequisite for a clear sense of doctrine; unless we are in Christ, we will not grasp the depth of our belonging to God as his children. But, Jesus also deals with our belonging to God in terms of a wonderful attachment to the Father. He points out very clearly that, "I am the vine, and my Father is the vinedresser. Every branch of mine that does not bear fruit he takes away, and every branch that does bear fruit he prunes, that it may bear more fruit. . . . Abide in me, and I in you. As the branch cannot bear fruit by itself, unless it abides in the vine, neither can you, unless you abide in me. I am the vine; you are the branches. Whoever abides in me and I in him, he it is that bears much fruit, for apart from me you can do nothing" (John 15:1-2, 4-5). Here I see that the real source of wisdom comes from that relationship with the Lord Jesus Christ.

If we talk about wars among the people of God; much of it is because of this lack of fellowship with the Lord. When there is no vital communion between the person and the Lord, there is no life and no peace along with it. Interpersonal quarrels, inner personal fights and anxieties are all the result of lack of wisdom from above. Here we see the bridge of that lack of wisdom to a new territory that is the main highway to constant communion with God: Prayer.

Lack of Wisdom Brings Forth Inner Emptiness

We often hear people say that we humans have a vacuum that has the shape of God. I do not understand it much, except that what I believe they are saying is that the emptiness that we have before believing in Christ seems to be completely filled with the presence of the Lord in our lives. Philosophically, this is acceptable; but theologically, I have my doubts. God is bigger than that vacuum, vacuum is shapeless and God has the desire to restore a broken relationship, not to fill what we think it is our own shapeless empty existence. There is, however, a number of figures of speech that seem to help this understanding from another angle. Our Lord Jesus often spoke of our thirst and our hunger, for example. The real issue here, as I see it, is that we continue to walk without having a number of things in our lives because of our lack of wisdom. James tackles this issue in a rather negative way, "You want something but don't get it. You kill and covet, but you cannot have what you want. You quarrel and fight. You do not have, because you do not ask God" (v. 2).

Humans have a deep hunger for something that ultimately would fulfill their lives. Their emptiness is so great that it looks like a bottomless well. This is the main characteristic of anybody who is manipulated by envy, lust and selfish ambition. Perhaps some of you will remember a pop song by the Rolling Stones titled "Satisfaction." It starts by saying, "I can get no satisfaction." This is the cry of millions of people who have everything but at the same time lack every meaningful thing for their own lives. This kind of emptiness can be easily illustrated by the enormous influence of advertising in the world. It is no wonder the extremely high cost of a minute of a commercial during the Super Bowl, for example. The return is even higher. Two quick examples will suffice: the first is related to our natural desire for food. It is appealing to see a juicy hamburger on the TV screen just before the 11:00 PM news. You will be somehow conditioned to have that the next day, when you feel hungry. I fell to that scheme a couple of weeks ago: I saw a new juicy hamburger ad from Carl's Jr. I told my wife that I wanted to have it for lunch the next day. We went out and I drove all the way to Jack in the Box, sure that the place was Carl's Jr. The funny situation is that since the night before I was absolute sure of the place, except that we do not have any Carl's Jr. in town. The power of suggestion. The second illustration has to do with fashion. We are still in the middle of winter and all the magazines are already showing the summer collection. I am a plain Jeans kind of guy, but suddenly I came to the realization that I have a lot of clothes that I even do not wear any more. I realized that a person like me lives with very few clothes in his closet. In one of my trips to Russia, I took more clothes than I really needed there; the one lesson I learned: The amount of money I paid for the excess weight was enough to buy any amount of clothes that I really needed there, under the Siberian Winter. I would have profited more just by not taking a lot of clothes with me and then buying the ones I really needed there instead. After learning my lesson, I started to do it differently: I now take brand new clothes with me on my next trips. Thus, when I go to teach in Mozambique, Angola, and other developing countries, I leave my clothes for the seminary students in those places.

"You kill and covet," shows that such a person is breaking the complete law of God. To *kill* (there is some dispute on the word *kill* or *envy*, but it has not been settled by any scholar yet) reminds the words of Jesus Christ in the Sermon on the Mount (Matthew 5:21-24). And to *covet* reminds the Apostle Paul when he ends up saying that once you break this commandment, you have broken the whole law, because it is the only inwardly commandment in the Ten Commandments, the Tenth Commandment (Romans 6-7). This is another side of this unfortunate state before the Lord. We tend to always look over to the greener grass on our neighbor's backyard. Again, we tend to covet the things that others have and we don't. It is simply pitiful, really pathetic! But it is part of our miserable life, because of lack of wisdom. No need to comment on this. You are guilty, I am guilty. The very moment we lack God's wisdom, we fall into that same trap all the time. This goes in all directions, in all areas of our lives.

"But you cannot have what you want." Even though they try hard to get some favor (mercy) from God, they will not receive a thing. People who are not right before the Lord will not receive from God any favor — we are reminded, however, that to be right before

The Wisdom Of James

the Lord is made possible only through Jesus Christ, our Mediator (our High Priest, according to Hebrews). They may fight and quarrel as much as they want, but this will not produce any response from above. William Gurnall puts it this way, "The jealousies and fears we entertain in our tempted souls disparage the mercy of God, because they have no foundation in the Divine nature."

"You do not have, because you do not ask God." This is how James tells his congregation that they in fact do not pray to God to ask him for the many blessings that are available to the children of God. We live in an age of distress and hurry. There is little commitment to prayer. That is why so many of us are suffering without any reason. We may find time for everything but prayer. The priorities seem to have changed and the spiritual things are put aside as a secondary issue in our busy lives (because we are children of a rather materialistic and technological society).

I am aware that God is able to give us anything we need without us "bothering" him in prayer. He is sovereign and he knows everything. But if he did so, he would do for us more than he did for his only Son Jesus who was always praying; even few hours before his death he was in prayer at the Gethsemane Garden. Richard Lovelace writes, "In the late twentieth century the race is not being won by the brilliant or the well organized. Pentecostals have become a 'third force' in world Christianity, not because their doctrine is perfect, but because they have prayer. If we are to be delivered from attempting only what is predictably achievable, we must return to a proper regard for prayer. To quote the great missionary leader, William Carey, we must 'expect great things from God and attempt great things for God.'"

Another Christian has come to the same conclusion, "Pentecostal churches have grown as they have not because their brilliance or the doctrine or their organization but because the Lord honors people and churches who pray. 'You have not because you ask not.'"

Lack of Wisdom Brings Forth Wrong Motives

There is nothing more disturbing than talking with Christians who have been bought into the unbiblical theology of prosperity.

The Wisdom Of James

The jargon of "name it and claim it" is very appealing, but soundly unbiblical. I heard one of their advocates give a series of teachings on how to have a lot of things through prayer. She was proudly telling her audience of how many new dresses she now has just because she keeps praying to God to have them because, in her words, she deserves it. Her main argument is that, as a child of the King, she deserves the best and we all are the children of the King for that matter. That particular lady used this very text of James, but she never mentioned verse 3, not once. She always stopped at the end of verse 2, "You do not have, because you do not ask." Fair enough, but James has in his teaching another part of the Scripture that shows that there were among his parishioners those who did not have it because they asked with the wrong motives, "When you ask, you do not receive, because you ask with wrong motives, that you may spend what you get on your pleasures" (v. 3).

When finally some of the members of St. James church asked something, they asked with the wrong motivation. This is very common even today. We find among ourselves a great deal of people who ask God for things that he will never consider giving to them. There is a very interesting illustration in the life of the late Norman Vincent Peale, during his childhood, which taught him a lesson on prayer,

Norman had been urged by a friend to experiment with smoking. He had a cigar and had gone into the kitchen to get some matches, planning then to meet his friend and smoke. His parents had specifically told him not to smoke, but he was determined to give it a try. He was holding the cigar in his hand and looking through a kitchen drawer for matches when his father surprised him. Immediately Norman turned around holding the cigar behind him, hoping his father hadn't seen it. He thought fast and said, "Hi, Dad. There's something I wanted to ask you." "What is it, son?" "Dad, will you take me to the circus next month?" Norman said he never forgot his Dad's reply. His Dad said, "Son, don't stand there in the act of disobedience and expect me to grant your request" (Quoted by John Bristol, Milpitas, California, c. 1987).

I once met a young lady in Southern California who hated God and did not want to become a Christian. The reason was that God did not give her a motorcycle so she could travel with her peers. I have no doubt that the problem was not to ask for a motorcycle, I have been riding motorcycles for a number of years, I am part of the Christian Motorcyclists Association, and I prayed about purchasing my motorcycle. I have met and ridden with a number of dear brothers and sisters who enjoy that sport and also use their talents and gifts to evangelize other bikers around the Northwest United States. The young lady I met in Southern California was just asking for that motorcycle with the wrong motive. I hope she has changed her heart and that she is now riding her bike, but with the right motive, of course. This reminds me of an old tune by Janis Joplin:

Oh Lord, won't you buy me a Mercedes Benz?
My friends all drive Porches, I must make amends.
Worked hard all my lifetime, no help from my friends,
So Lord, won't you buy me a Mercedes Benz?

I may be biased in showing examples that are only related to physical things; I may be guilty in this area, of course. Physical things, however, are tangible ways to show what is in our deepest and innermost feelings. There are several prayers that are completely against God's moral law and related to very intimate and personal issues that go beyond the desire of getting something physical. Sometimes we ask God for things that do not glorify his name. We must always look into his word to find the necessary wisdom to know his will for us. It is okay to make a wish list, but we must surrender it to God's will. The very first question we must ask is the simplest one: Lord, will this bring glory to your name?

"Because you ask with wrong motives." The sole motive for asking God in prayer is to glorify his name above all names. Every human being has a deep need for God. Back to what I addressed at the top of this chapter, as someone once said, "We have a Christ-shaped vacuum that only the Lord Jesus can satisfy." There is absolutely nothing that can fulfill any man's heart with happiness, but Jesus Christ. It reminds of the history of Howard Hughes, one of the richest men in the last century. Apparently he could not find happiness. The way of his passing from here to eternity seems to have demonstrated that. Only Jesus Christ can fill the emptiness of someone's heart. "I have come that they may have life, and have it to the full" (John 10:10). History is filled with examples like that. Another historical figure that often comes to my mind is that of the French philosopher Jean Paul Sartre, whose death depicted the core of his own view on life.

"That you may spend what you get on your pleasures." That is the same idea behind the story of the Prodigal Son, "and there squandered his wealth in wild living" (Luke 15:13). Again, Gurnall puts it this way, "Mercies ill gotten are commonly ill spent because they are not sanctified to them, and thus become fuel to feed their lusts."

As we conclude this chapter, I want to emphasize that lack of wisdom will produce all the "lacks" in our lives, because it has its origin in earthly things, in our unspiritual hearts, and it comes from the devil. This will make our lives simply deplorable.

The test of our prayer lives will show evidences of how God is pleased to give us his many blessings: "You do not have, because you do not ask God." We are here reminded once more of God's favor and love for us. If we ask with wisdom, we will receive anything we ask because our petition will honor him. Again, "Every good and perfect gift is from above, coming down from the Father or the heavenly lights, who does not change like shifting shadows" (1:17). May the Holy Name of our Lord be glorified through our prayer life; we are able to accomplish great things for him if we have a prayer life that is watered with wisdom. To him be all the glory forever and ever! Amen.

Chapter 12

The Secret of Walking with God: The Test of Humility

James 4:4-12

The fourth chapter of James talks about several dangers that the Christian faces in life: Human passions (1-10); Evil speaking (11-12), and Rash confidence (13-17). We saw in the last chapter one of the tests that this chapter brings to us, the test of prayer, which was related to the problem of wrong motives. Those motives are generated primarily by our selfishness, our inability of looking beyond ourselves and our own needs. Basically, James wants to show in this chapter two key thoughts, both of them in opposition to each other: *Pride* (or arrogance) and *Humbleness* (or humility). Our response to either or both depends on how we have apprehended the wisdom that comes from above, from God.

We live in a world of self promotion. The more you "sell" yourself, the more money or success you have a chance of obtaining. Competition is fierce. We see how the world manipulates the shape of success and how it dictates the core of the rat race that becomes a highway to nothingness and disillusion in the end of the day. The world has no notion of what it is to be humble; pride is the word of the day. We see for example the massive "Gay Pride" parades around the world. At the time of this writing, the gay parade in São Paulo gathered over 1.4 million people; this same week, major cities of the world also had their "pride parade": Paris, Madrid, Vancouver, among them. The terms "pride," "proud," "prideful" are used as part of the affirmation of one's lack of self affirmation. When a person wants to stand out in any situation, social status or business, she or he usually would say, "I am proud of ..." In some ways, this reminds me of the Babel Tower; I just do not know how to explain it in a few words. I do not want to enter in a battle over the semantics behind the term, but I want to draw your attention to the dangers of misplaced self-affirmation.

James is not wrong when he links wrongful prayer requests to the whole issue of pride and arrogance. They usually go together. In one sense, people who come to God with their wrong requests, they do so because they simply do not want to humble themselves before the Lord. There is such a thing as the arrogance of being "children of God." Also, the arrogance of thinking that because you are a child of God you have the right to demand from him whatever you want. This is just what the brother of Jesus did not want to see happening to his churches. That's why we see the link between prayer and attitude in this passage; but also, the lack of understanding about the sovereign love of God and also his judicial role.

This chapter deals with yet another test in our faith: the test of humility. The question to this problem is pointed at the very beginning: How do I respond to God's wisdom in relationship to my Christian witness? It is a rather practical question indeed. It has, however, a lot to offer in terms of how we are expected to act in reference to what we claim to believe. This passage will lead us to underscore our walk with the Lord; that is, it will help us to better understand our fellowship with God.

Walk in Friendship with God

The text mentions fights, quarrels, envy, lust, enmity with God, and so on. All of these are related to our "friendship with the world." A word must be said about the term "World." In this context, it seems to mean "The whole system of humanity (its institutions, structures, values and mores) as organized without God." In other words, anything that does not come or include God is in this category.

The Wisdom Of James

Much has been written about the "World" and its relationship between God and humans. On the one hand, the Bible teaches that "God so loved the world" (John 3:16). In that context, we see that God loves the people who live in the world; which is the stage where God sends his Son Jesus Christ to redeem those who have been lost in their sins and trespasses. On the other hand, Paul admonishes us that we should have a new mindset, acquire a new world view and not allow the world to continue to shape our way of thinking (cf. Romans 12:2). John uses the same word to par with Paul and James, "Do not love the world or the things in the world. If anyone loves the world, the love of the Father is not in him. For all that is in the world—the desires of the flesh and the desires of the eyes and pride in possessions—is not from the Father but is from the world. And the world is passing away along with its desires, but whoever does the will of God abides forever" (1 John 2:15-17). In this passage, we see the definition of the term "world" and how it differs from what God has intended for his children.

James goes as far as to say that to love this world is indeed enmity with God. He uses a very hard expression: those Christians who change allegiance, betray God and are compared to "adulterous people." James uses his argument like the Old Testament did in the past (e.g.: Hosea 1:2; 4:12; Isaiah 54:5). Here he is dealing with spiritual infidelity. It was a terminology that the Jewish believers would understand because this is how God treated Israel every time she betrayed him. Jesus also used this same characterization for the spiritually infidel, calling them "adulterous generation." "An evil and adulterous generation seeks for a sign, but no sign will be given to it except the sign of Jonah" (Matthew 16:4). Later in his ministry, he again addresses the crowd and his disciples, after foretelling his death and resurrection, with these words, "For whoever is ashamed of me and of my words in this adulterous and sinful generation, of him will the Son of Man also be ashamed when he comes in the glory of his Father with the holy angels" (Mark 8:38). This also reminds us of him when he taught that one cannot serve two masters at the same time (Matthew 6:24).

Lehman Strauss describes the spiritually adulterous person with force, "The Christian who turns from Christ and his Church to seek pleasure and satisfaction at the cisterns of this world are like unfaithful women who leave their husbands to seek sensual pleasure with other men. God is jealous over us with a holy jealousy. He purchased us at great sacrifice to Himself; hence he wants us solely for Himself."

The issue of enmity with God has created several positions in relation to the Christian religion over the years. Some have gone to either one extreme or the other. There are some who have rejected the world completely, hiding themselves in total isolation. Those are the ones who take the position that God is completely against the world. There are others, however, who think that God works within the world and therefore live lives that show no difference between believers and non-believers having a religion that is rather syncretistic. There are yet others who think that God is above the world (i.e., above the culture; or meta-cultural). He does not endorse the world but transforms it by the power of his kingdom. This seems to be the position that Jesus Christ taught and continues doing over the centuries in order to advance his kingdom on earth.

But the passage we are now studying talks about having friendship with God. The only way for that friendship is to hate the world. A lot has been taught by Jesus about this very issue of love and hate; or, of prioritizing our center of affection. He taught that we should love him more than everything; with such a love that anything else would look like complete hatred (Luke 14:25-33). Instead of seeking the pleasures of the world, he taught us to seek his kingdom and his justice as the one priority of our lives (Matthew 6:33). It is in the midst of his suffering, just before he was taken to the cross that he commanded his disciples to love each other and then he links that with the issue of friendship by saying, "You are my friends if you do what I command you" (John 15:14). Later on, he continued to say that because his disciples will love him and love each other, the world will hate them (John 15:18-19).

Paul talks about our restored friendship with God (Romans 5:1-12). It is based on his love for us (also, John 15:13) and such new friendship is to be nourished and is expected to grow. A new friendship is the most precious gift one could have; it brings new life, a new hope that will keep on forever. But that friendship is also

The Wisdom Of James

based on mutuality; the worst thing in a friendship is when there is a communication breakdown or an act of betrayal. This is what James was talking to his brothers and sisters: wisdom from heaven preserves friendship with God.

Two things are most important at this moment in order to enhance our friendship with God. The first one is *time in prayer*. Kistemaker points it out in this way, "The sin of failing to come to God in prayer is one of the most common offenses a Christian commits." Prayer was a reality beyond comprehension for the followers of Jesus in the early days. They knew that he was alive; many of them had walked with him when he was among them in Israel. They knew that God was alive and that Jesus was their Mediator between them and the Father; as Paul points out that there is only one mediator between us, the man Jesus Christ (1 Timothy 2:5). We somehow need to be reminded over and over again of this reality for today. We worship a living God, a living Father who cares for us and who is our friend. It is through his Son Jesus Christ that we have full access to him (Hebrews 10:19-22).

The second is to spend *time with his Word*. A person must spend time in the Scripture. It is there that we will find all we need to live a life that is full of blessings and that will honor him. The Word of God is the most precious form of communication that we have from the Lord besides his Son Jesus Christ, who is the full expression of God's revelation to us (Hebrews 1:1-3). It is in his Word that we find the road map for our lives; it is there that we read about his love for each one of the elect, the faithful remnant that will one day be with him forever in the new Earth.

In sum, the great blessing that comes from walking in friendship with God is simply to be called *a friend of God*, as Abraham was called (mentioned in Isaiah 41 and James 2). In that same way, Jesus Christ said that "you are my friends if you do what I command." In order to have a friend in Jesus, we need to walk with his Father.

Walk Humbly With God

The most noted trait in the lives of those who do not walk with the Lord is their pride, their arrogance. We see it in two ways: First,

141

when one becomes selfish, self-sufficient and proud (all are synonymous in one way or the other); acting this way leads us to neglect God as our Lord and Helper. The more arrogant one becomes the more one thinks he or she does not need God. An example of this was found by a colleague of mine working in a Kibbutz in Israel a few years ago. He witnessed many of its dwellers saying that it was not God who built that particular Kibbutz, but their own hands. A famous singer from my home country, Elis Regina, upon entering her condominium certain evening, told the porter, "nobody is to bother me, not even God." She was found dead the next morning in her bedroom. I do not think God killed her because of what she said, but we may say that there was a metaphoric ending to her life. She was a well liked personality and that incident brought a great distress to millions of people in the days that followed her demise.

I had the sadness of watching the fall of a colleague of mine a number of years ago. He comes from a humble family and was brought up in the ways of the Lord since childhood. At the age of seventeen, he was to be considered a phenomenon in his knowledge of the Scriptures. I remember a number of times when he led intricate Bible studies to our youth group and he did not even have any notes in front of him, just his Bible. Years went by and he went to seminary, he graduated a year after me. He was ordained to the ministry of the Gospel and became the senior pastor of a major church in Brazil. But there was something that most people started to see in him: his pride and arrogance. I was already in the United States when I received information that he had succumbed to sin. Many colleagues of ours tried to help him, but that was completely in vain. In my last trip to Brazil, I learned that that once humble person, because of his arrogance later, is now completely outside the church, living as a completely unsaved person. This true story reminds me of yet another one; this time found in the Bible: the story of King Saul. A man who started his life as a very humble man and came to his last day in a miserable death because of his arrogance. Proverbs teaches us that "Towards the scorners he is scornful, but to the humble he gives favor" (Proverbs 3:34). Hundreds of years later, James takes this same passage from its Greek translation, the Septuagint, and includes it in his epistle, "God opposes the proud, but gives grace to the humble" (4:6). Grace is not for the prideful, but for the humble; or, in Jesus' teaching, to the poor in spirit, the meek, the ones who mourn and hope for justice (cf. Matthew 5:1-12).

The way of humbleness is shown in this passage. In order to walk in humility before the Lord we are to recognize these steps. First, the text tells us to submit ourselves to God and resist the devil; second, we are told to come near to God and he will come near to us. This requires a complete change in our lifestyle. Psalm 24:3-4 helps us to understand what is at stake here, "Who may ascend the hill of the Lord? Who may stand in his holy place? He who has clean hands and a pure heart, who does not lift up his soul to an idol, or swear by what is false." Other passages that will help us in a better understanding of this attitude of humbleness and our need to be found pure before the Lord show that once we are redeemed by the blood of Jesus Christ we have a new life and, because of that, we are to walk in holiness. The Lord said, "Be holy, for I am holy" (Leviticus 11:44). Peter, using the same passage, calls the churches in the Diaspora to be likewise (1 Peter 1:13-16). Paul, calling Timothy to have a life of prayer, reminds us that, "I desire then that in every place the men should pray, lifting holy hands without anger or quarreling" (1 Timothy 2:8).

This attitude goes beyond external clean hands, however. The Lord Jesus Christ, quoting the Prophet Isaiah, goes to the center of the problem. It resides in the hearts of the people: true relationship with God comes from a true act of worship. Talking about traditions and commandments, the Lord reminds those in his audience that God sees the heart of the worshiper: "'You hypocrites! Well did Isaiah prophesy of you, when he said: "This people honors me with their lips, but their heart is far from me; in vain do they worship me, teaching as doctrines the commandments of men"'" (Matthew 15:7-9). The relation of this passage to what Jesus told the Samaritan woman is very close. He told that woman that time would come when we would worship God in spirit and in truth (John 4:23).

We are called to repentance with a sincere attitude of sorrow before the Lord. "Grieve, mourn and wail. Change your laughter to mourning and your joy to gloom" (v. 9). Also, we find Paul's admonition in this important part of Scripture, "Godly sorrow brings repentance that leads to salvation and leaves no regret, but worldly sorrow brings death" (2 Corinthians 7:10). James deals with a philosophical adversity, it seems. He is saying that even our laughter should be transformed into mourning and that our joy should be turned to gloom (v. 9). He is making sure that his audience grasp the real meaning of true repentance. It is true that salvation brings joy, but that joy will come after a night of sorrow for what we have done and what we need to repent of, as we may read in Psalm 30:5, "Weeping may tarry for the night, but joy comes with the morning." But here, James is calling the Church to a time of great sorrow, of true repentance. Strauss puts it this way, "The chastening of our own hearts because of our sin is not provocative of careless laughter. Mourning and heaviness always accompany a deep sense of sin. The Bible is the most joyful Book in the world, and Christianity the most joyful religion, but the real abiding joy of the cleansed and forgiven sinner can come only after deep sorrow for sin."

This reminds me of a small sign at an AA meeting place that I visited in Russia a few years ago. Speaking with the director in charge, he told me the story behind that sign: although the former alcoholic rejoices in the new found freedom in Christ, she or he will often be reminded of the times of great sorrow that have been part of their lives. This is the saying in the sign: "Please Lord teach us to laugh again but, God don't ever let us forget that we cried."

The attitude of sorrow or repentance is the most evident demonstration of true revival throughout Church history. Any reading of the history of revivals will show us that they came to fruition when people were seeking the Lord in prayer and also when the Holy Spirit visited their lives bringing forth the sorrow that brings repentance. We find hear the evidence of revival and we should expect it to come to us when we come to the Lord in humble attitude of confession of our sins and a sincere demonstration of how sorrow we are for what we have done. Only then the mercies of the Lord will be poured down on us.

Walk in Fear of God's Judgment

If in chapter 3 James talks about the tongue and the issue of false teaching, here in chapter 4 he deals with the issue of slandering, which is more personal, that is, more individual. Slandering may destroy great friendships, it may destroy many good relationships in our lives and in our communities. He mentions the need to control our tongues in chapters 1 and 3, but here the tone of what he wants to convey is more directly linked to the malicious faultfinding that a believer may have against the other. In this case, it is related with judging one another without any basis for such.

The issue of judging another person requires special attention. It can come in various ways, but in most cases its source is anger, frustration, envy, prejudice, fear or simply lack of love. The teachings of Jesus will help the believer not to judge one another. The Lord teaches in Matthew 7 that before we go about judging anyone else, we must first judge ourselves. He is not saying that we should not judge a person, but that we must first find out that we are all imperfect and that we have faults that may be much bigger than the ones we are trying to see in the other person. If someone has anything offensive against you, the Lord teaches that we should go to that person and try to clarify things with him or her: "If your brother sins against you, go and tell him his fault, between you and him alone. If he listens to you, you have gained your brother. But if he does not listen, take one or two others along with you, that every charge may be established by the evidence of two or three witnesses. If he refuses to listen to them, tell it to the church" (Matthew 18:15-17a). Here we see that there is a place in our relationships for sound judgment, but not as a form of slander; rather, as an attempt to gain the person over that particular issue.

Another way of seeing the concept of judgment is found in Paul's teaching to the Corinthians. He calls the church in Corinth to make an evaluation among themselves whether or not they are in Christ: "Examine yourselves, to see whether you are in the faith. Test yourselves. Or do you not realize this about yourselves, that Jesus Christ is in you?—unless indeed you fail to meet the test! I hope you will find out that we have not failed the test" (2 Corinthians 13:5-6). John, in the same Spirit, calls the Church to judge for themselves who is from God or not: "Beloved, do not believe every spirit, but test the spirits to see whether they are from God, for many false prophets have gone out into the world" (1 John 4:1). I should say that here the problem is related to the issue of doctrine and of sound teaching in the Church. It is also related to the issue of firm and honest relationships between the church and the prophet, pastor, or apostle, which was the case of Paul and the church in Corinth. We live in a society that has misappropriated the idea of judgment and has misused the teachings of Jesus Christ and of the Apostles for their own benefit. This has to do with many who want to live sinful lifestyles and do not want to hear the truth about their sin; therefore, they launch in the conversation the one passage they have memorized for their own profit: Matthew 7:1-5.

Another problem with judgment comes in the realm of prejudices. Paul deals with this issue in two passages: Romans 14-15 and part of 1 Corinthians 8. It is related to people who are considered to be weak in their faith. This is an interesting phenomenon in the Church: there is a number of people who have not grown enough in their faith to understand some aspects of that new found faith. Others, who have already walked a few miles ahead should respect them and treat them with love and consideration. In many cases, this is the worst form of self-righteous judgment over those who are not there yet. We should refrain from that sin. Another prejudicial form of sin is addressed by James (2:1-13), when he talks about those who despise the poor to give more attention to the rich.

The Church of today has suffered from this same kind of prejudicial judgment. There seems to be a double standard between one faction of the Church and another. Speaking from a Latin American perspective, I have experienced a number of instances happening to me and my fellow Latinos. It is sad to see that we are frequently seen as second class citizens not only in the market place but also in the Church.

But James, I want to remind the reader, is dealing here with the sin of faultfinding, the sin of slandering against other brothers and sisters. Here we may find some of the dangers of slandering: First, it separates close friends. The Bible has this to say, "He who covers

The Wisdom Of James

an offense promotes love, but whoever repeats the matter separates close friends" (Proverbs 17:9). I have encountered numerous cases of people who have destroyed long time friendships because of an evil word against the other. It hurts people and brings no glory to the Lord.

The second danger is even more severe. By judging the Law, one is judging God: "There is only one Law-giver and Judge, the one who is able to save and destroy" (v. 12). James is admonishing against the danger of judging the Royal Law, the Law of Love (2:8). By doing so, the believer is judging not the law but the One who gave us that law: God Himself. We are reminded then that there is only one Judge. Jesus said, "The Father judges no one, but has given all judgment to the Son, that all may honor the Son, just as they honor the Father" (John 5:22). Then, Paul, writing to the Romans, has something to say to them. Some scholars believe that one of the main reasons Paul wrote to the Romans is that they, being themselves Gentiles, were putting down the Jewish believers. So Paul, talking about their unhealthy way of judging their Jewish brothers and sisters, adds the following word, "Why do you pass judgment on your brother? Or you, why do you despise your brother? For we all will stand before the judgment seat of God" (Romans 14:10).

We are reminded over and over again that *all of us* will appear before the judgment seat of Jesus in that Great Day. There will be no escape for arrogant people; for some, it will be a glorious day, but for others, it will be a dreadful day. "For we must all appear before the judgment seat of Christ, that each one may receive what is due him for the things done while in the body, whether good or bad" (2 Corinthians 5:10).

We are called by God to humbly walk in his presence. There is not a single instance in the entire Scripture that shows that the proud, the arrogant of this world will have the blessing of walking with the Lord. This leads me to one of the most intriguing instances in Jesus' ministry: the dispute among the disciples to see who among them would be regarded as the greatest. Jesus turned to them and said, "The kings of the Gentiles exercise lordship over them, and those in authority over them are called benefactors. But not so with you. Rather, let the greatest among you become as the youngest,

The Wisdom Of James

and the leader as one who serves. For who is the greater, one who reclines at the table or one who serves? Is it not the one who reclines at the table? But I am among you as the one who serves" (Luke 22:24-27).

"Humble yourselves before the Lord, and he will exalt you" (v. 10). I have learned two important things during my growing up in Brazil: the first is related to the fall of the proud. We learned that the higher the proud person flies, the harder will their fall be. But also, I learned about a disease that the proud have: "Balloonites." The proud is always full of air; it takes just a small pin to blow him up. How sad! This is very true. The "taller" the person is at his own sight, the smaller that person is at the sight of God. The true giant in the Kingdom of God is the dwarf, not the other way around.

I would like to end this chapter with an anecdote, it happened to me a number of years ago in Southern California. I was a young missionary, raising support in order to go to France. In one of my duties, I was sent to a major Sunday School Conference at a large church in Anaheim as a representative of my mission organization. It was about six o'clock in the evening and I was sitting by my booth when I noticed a gentleman approaching it. He was a person no different to anybody else that I know. He stroke a conversation with me, demonstrating a genuine interest in what I was doing and mostly on the great need in France for new Evangelical missionaries. The gentleman was dressed very casually, had a very humble spirit and a demonstration of profound love for Jesus Christ. Back in my mind, I was just thinking about what church he might be a member and how blessed that church was. Just before he left, he shook my hands and introduced himself: "Ehud, I'm glad to have met you. My name is Bill Bright." He was the main speaker for that evening…

Chapter 13

Deo Volente! Submission to God's Will

James 4:13-17

Show me, O LORD, my life's end and the number of my days; let me know how fleeting is my life. You have made my days a mere handbreadth; the span of my years is as nothing before you. Each man's life is but a breath. Man is a mere phantom as he goes to and fro: He bustles about, but only in vain; he heaps up wealth, not knowing who will get it. (King David, Psalm 39:4-6)

James advances his line of thought to the crux of his teaching in the Episple's fourth chapter: the will of God. The topic of God's will is not a very popular one, even in church circles. Much has been said about it and somehow people are under the impression that the will of God must first match our own will. If it goes somewhat differently, God's will is soon disregarded. It sounds a little dramatic at first, but this truth is present in our daily lives. The sad news is that we, including myself, are quick to ignore God's will as if we have any control over our lives. But we forget that the Lord has always the best for his children. A good way to start the day should be to remind ourselves that God works everything for the good of

The Wisdom Of James

those whom he loves and has a purpose for them (cf. Romans 8:28). With that in mind, we turn to this third part of chapter 4 of James.

Peter Davids includes this passage as part one of two other tests. He suggests that this passage is the "test of wealth," whereas 5:1-6 is the "test by the wealthy." I see where he might be going with his personal division of the book, but I continue to believe that this passage is part of the entire chapter 4, being that in here James is calling his readers to realize the danger of ignoring God in their decision making. It is not difficult to see that the chapter has three significant emphases, but all of them have everything to do with lack of wisdom. Moreover, all of them have deep roots in arrogance and contempt.

We have the opportunity of making plans for our lives; in fact, most of us have a purpose statement since we were children. Some want to pursue a career in the military, others want to become athletes, others want to be lawyers, and so forth. This is a noble motivation in our hearts, and we should pursue those dreams. I am personally grateful to the Lord for our brother Rick Warren and his bestseller purpose-driven books and ministry. There is nothing wrong with having a mission statement or a long term plan of action; on the contrary, we learn from God himself that the universe is not a purposeless creation. God, like a wise Architect, designed the entire creation, as we may find in Proverbs 8:22-31, for instance. The entire message in the Bible shows that God followed a plan that he, in his omniscience, decreed to happen before he said the very first word of creation, "Let there be light!" (Genesis 1:3). As we will learn, we will succeed in those plans that we make for the glory of God. I once heard a pastor say that "A man only hits what he aims for." Very true! To aim for some important goal is a noble thing to do. But here we are going to deal with what goes beyond just aiming for something.

Even the Apostle Paul had his own mission statement, which should be not only an inspiration for us but also a normative teaching from the Holy Spirit for our lives. Here is how he redirected his entire life after he had his personal encounter with Jesus Christ, "I want to know Christ and the power of his resurrection and the fellowship of sharing in his sufferings, becoming like him in his death, and so, somehow, to attain to the resurrection from the dead" (Philippians 3:10-11).

Unexpected Moments in Our Lives

Many of you have heard about Murphy's Law and how things may happen to people. My wife chastises me sometimes because I keep referring to my "lack of luck" in grocery stores, for example; it "never" fails me: "every time" I choose a line with one or two people in front of me, the next person either has a problem with her or his debit card, a merchandise does not have the right price in it, and so forth. So I have now decided that I will choose the longer lines instead. In a negative way, we are confronted with unexpected things to happen and there is nothing we can do about them. A friend of mine has something to say about his honeymoon. Everything that could go wrong happened to him in Hawaii: he got sick with the flu, his credit and debit cards were stolen in the airport, two of their pieces of luggage ended up in Korea, and when he finally got better from his flu, his bride got it. By that time, they had to come home. These incidents are circumstantial and as much part of our daily lives as we can expect. They keep us humble and, of course, they help to shape our sense of humor.

But there are incidents that come to us in ways that will change the course of our lives. "Eric," left for the United States to pursue a doctorate in chemistry, along with his loving wife, "Florinda," and their two little children. They went to live in a prominent city in the South, where he attended school. His Ph.D. program took him and his family to other parts of the world as he did his research: England, Germany, Belgium, Israel, and Japan. An accomplished student, before his graduation he had received several high paying job offers from organizations in Japan, Italy and Argentina. Because he was under a grant program from Brazil, Eric had to return to his country for at least five years in order to comply with the terms of that scholarship. Eric was an elder in his church and was always telling others how much he was looking forward to resuming his service in that community of faith. Graduation came and he was granted the highest honor in his area of research. A day after his graduation, while preparing to take his family to Orlando, along with his parents, for a week of celebration, Eric fell sick. Two days later, he was with the Lord. The one question at the time, in the middle of so much sadness and pain, was about the purpose of his life and why had he to die at such a young age. We see that in God's mind and purpose, nothing is lost; we just cannot fathom the extent of his plans for us. This chapter talks about purposes, plans, and dreams. It also talks about the brevity of life, as we could see in this story.

As we continue, we will realize that there is, also, another way of making plans; and that one does not honor God. This is what James is addressing in this passage. Again, he continues to talk about the secret of walking with the Lord. We learned in the last chapter that we should walk with the Lord in friendship, in humility, and in fear of the Lord's judgment. Now, we will study another important secret, and that is the secret of walking in submission to God's will. Here is what James sees as a very key element for a victorious life in our daily walk with the Lord. As we learn to include—better yet, to acknowledge the Lord in our lives—we will surrender ourselves to his loving care on a continuous basis. This is the test of submission to God's will.

Self-Centered Decision Making

"Now listen, you who say, 'Today or tomorrow we will go to this or that city, spend a year there, carry on business and make money. Why, you do not even know what will happen tomorrow'" (vv.13-14a). Apparently James was addressing the merchants who belonged or not to the Christian church of his time. They were arrogant merchants who were making plans for the future without counting on God's sovereign grace and providence. John Calvin makes a comment on this passage and points out that, "James roused the stupidity of those who disregarded God's providence, and claimed for themselves a whole year, though they had not a single moment in their own power." Strauss makes an important note on the sentiment behind the attitude of those who were making their plans, "A common sin is dealt with here. It is that of practical atheism, planning without taking God into account. Here are those who plan their lives as if their own wills were final and supreme. . . . This is bold human presumption giving no thought whatever to divine providence."

The Word of God teaches us that we may make plans, but the final approval comes from the mouth of the Lord. We find a passage in Proverbs that makes it very clear, "To man belong the plans of the heart, but from the LORD comes the reply of the tongue" (Proverbs 16:1). It is important that we realize that to him belongs the future, not to us. In his providence we live and continue to live; it is the hand of the Lord that guides us in his purposes for our lives.

I cannot help but remind myself of the terrifying experience that I, along with a few million others, went through on October 17, 1989. The third game of the World Series between the San Francisco Giants and the Oakland A's in San Francisco was ready to start. As I was going to my work place in Milpitas that morning, I heard on the radio a person saying that "We are the best in the world. . . . Today every people in the world are looking at us." Obviously he was talking about the World Series. It was around 5:20 PM, the teams were ready to play ball, and the earthquake hit the whole area with a fierce and dreadful impact. Its epicenter was in Santa Cruz, not far from where my family and I were living at the time. That was for me a great illustration of what could happen in just a few seconds and only God was in control of it. My family and I were also in Pasadena when the January 1994 earthquake hit Southern California. Another reminder that our plans can change in just a few seconds. I remember days later a friend of mine at Fuller Seminary came to me and said, "Ehud, I grew up here in Los Angeles and I am forty-two years-old. I have never seen an earthquake like this before. I am still scared of what we went through. Imagine when the Big One hits the area! It will be a complete disaster for all of us."

We must learn a very important lesson in this teaching from James. It may come as a question to us now: Who are we to make plans and not consider the Lord as the center of our decision making? Only fools do that. It applies to every single decision we make in our lives. As we are going through a time when the cost of living is becoming more and more difficult, I keep observing the decisions of many in their plans for vacation, business, even for schooling.

One will not know for sure if he or she will be able to pay off their increasing debts; there seems to be a race against the impossible nowadays: people are buying indiscriminately and increasing their debt as if the world is up for closure. The housing situation in our country has hit a level of confusion never seen before; foreclosures are rampant because of lack of wise planning. In the great need to keep up with the Joneses, many young families are now owing an average of two and a half cars per car. Let me explain, even so briefly. I have met couples who have changed more than two cars in the past three years; every time they do so, they include the remaining debt of the previous cars in the new ones they just wanted to buy. Others are getting rid of their "gas hogs" in order to get a car that has a better gas consumption. In order to do that, they are losing so much money in the deals without noticing that what they are supposedly saving in gas, they have already lost in the loss of their equity. In most cases, I have observed that people just live out their half made plans to realize later that they are in a life situation that has no turning back. The only answer to this problem is to realize that we cannot afford making our plans without the Lord.

The Brevity of Life

How many left for work at the World Trade Center on September 11, 2001, knowing that they were going to enter history that day by shedding their own blood as martyrs? No one, I believe, knew that one of the most terrible terrorist attacks in history was going to take place that morning. The second part of James comment to his readers comes with a question and a philosophical insertion afterwards: "What is your life? You are a mist that happens for a little while and then vanishes." (v. 4b).

What is our life? It is a brief passage in the short span of time that God has allowed for us. It is short, unpredictable, and completely out of our control. Even people who try very hard to preserve their health could die at any moment. An epitaph in a cemetery in New England read: "That's what I expected, but not so soon." The Bible says that, "The LORD knows the days of the blameless" (Psalm 37:18a, ESV). Elsewhere we read that, "Your eyes saw my unformed substance;

in your book were written, every one of them, the days that were formed for me, when as yet there were none of them" (Psalm 139:16, ESV).

King Solomon collected a proverb that helps us visualize life in the context of what James is here posing before us, "Do not boas about tomorrow, for you do not know what a day may bring forth" (Proverbs 27:1). But also, we see how Jesus Christ deals with the issue of life as he taught about anxiety and worries. He was a realist and did not hide from his disciples that life is not so easy. This is how he describes "tomorrow," "Therefore do no worry about tomorrow, for tomorrow will worry about itself. Each day has enough trouble of its own" (Matthew 6:34). Another way of looking at life, as brief as it is, comes from a serious study on Ecclesiastes. Again King Solomon, or the Preacher, teaches about life's vanity and how we should look into it from a different angle. At the end of the day, he concludes his book by saying that, "Now all has been heard; here is the conclusion of the matter: Fear God and keep his commandments, for his is the whole duty of man" (Ecclesiastes 12:13).

But it is Moses who puts it in perspective when he prayed, "You sweep men away in the sleep of death; they are like the new grass of the morning—though in the morning it springs up new, by evening it is dry and withered" (Psalm 90:5-6). Life is short and in the hands of the Lord Almighty. Although "a thousand years in your sight are like a day that has just gone by, or like a watch in the night" (Psalm 90:4), we are reminded that our lives are just like a mist in the presence of God and that we may return to the dust from where we came in just a minute. Even so, he gives an idea of the days of a person's life, "The length of our days is seventy years—or eighty, if we have the strength; yet their span is but trouble and sorrow, for they quickly pass, and we fly away" (Psalm 90:10).

James wants us to realize that life does not belong to us; it belongs to God who is the Life Giver. He is the one who gives us the grace to go through this life in order to glorify his name. It is the Lord who is able to keep our lives or take them away. The Lord Jesus taught us many precious lessons about our lives, but one that lingers the most is that we cannot add once single day to our lives. Talking about being anxious, he once said, "Who of you by worrying can add a single hour to his life? Since you cannot do this very little thing, why do you worry about the rest?" (Luke 12:25-26). The other notorious teaching of Jesus comes in the form of a parable, the Parable of the Rich Fool (Luke 12:13-21). After the rich fool decided to store everything, the Lord said, "You fool! This very night your life will be demanded from you" (v. 20). Here we see how brief our lives might be! Again, linked to the previous point, this affirms what the Scripture says in Proverbs, "Do not boast about tomorrow, for you do not know what a day may bring forth" (Proverbs 27:1).

When we know how brief our life is, we realize that there must be a higher purpose for it. I know of a man who devoted his life to make money, get rich and provide for his wife and two daughters. He was a hard working man, having grown up in a very poor family, he was able to develop a very nice holding of businesses selling commercial trucks. He died of cancer at the age of fifty. Visiting with other mutual friends later, I came to know that his widow and daughters never loved him; all they cared about was the money and possessions that he left behind. It is a tragic ending for someone's life; what would be the epitaph on that man's tomb? As we contemplate the brevity of our life before we are called to be with the Lord, we should make a sober evaluation of our goals and purpose for living.

Submitting to God's Will

"Instead, you ought to say, 'If it is the Lord's will, we will live and do this or that.' As it is, you boast and brag. All such boasting is evil" (vv.15-16). As I mentioned before, the center of this passage is the will of God. One will understand it only when more is said about the Providence of God in our lives. It is not by chance that we are alive; it is not by chance, or fatality, that we go through trials and temptations. At the center of this concept we will realize that God has intended good for us all the time, even when we go through hardships. God meant good fortune even for the Hebrews in the exile. It is hard to see it that way, but he had a solid plan for his people during that time in the land of exile. This is how he put it in the mouth of the Prophet Jeremiah, "'For I know the plans I have for you,' declares the LORD, 'plans to prosper you and not to harm you, plans to give you hope and a future" (Jeremiah 29:11). God, in his mysterious ways, provides for those whom he loves. We must be open to his prompting in our lives, knowing that he intends to bestow blessings upon his people.

Nonetheless, it is often difficult to realize this truth. Our tendency of not trusting in the Lord comes primarily from our own fears and anxieties. Those who do not include God in their plans are in great sin. My understanding of this issue comes from the knowledge that we have the gift of faith given to us—otherwise we would not even believe in Christ for salvation—and such faith must bring forth complete trust in God's will for us. For those who are self-centered in their decision making, the obvious evidence of their sin is their arrogance and contempt against God. This reminds me the last verse of "Invictus," William Henley's famous poem:

> *It matters not how strait the gate,*
> *How charged with punishments the scroll,*
> *I am the master of my fate,*
> *I am the captain of my soul.*

The problem of not submitting to the will of God comes primarily from the struggle a person has in releasing control of himself and accepting the fact that the Lord will take charge. It is a common problem for all of us; unless we surrender ourselves completely to him, we cannot call him Lord. Here is the reason why James says that, "Instead, you ought to say, 'If it is the Lord's will, we will live and do this or that'" (v. 15).

An important lesson on this particular issue comes from the book of Acts. Paul, Silas and Timothy were trying to reach Asia, after they left Derbe and Lystra. In fact they had a plan. What seems to have been a good plan was not God's plan for that time. The text will explain itself, "And they went through the region of Phrygia and Galatia, having been forbidden by the Holy Spirit to speak the word in Asia. And when they had come up to Mysia, they attempted to go into Bithynia, but the Spirit of Jesus did not allow them" (Acts 16:6-7, ESV). Here we see that, although they had a plan, God forbade them to accomplish it. Instead, we will learn later, they receive a vision to go to Macedonia instead, and this is how the Gospel entered Europe. It was Paul's practice to submit his plans to God's will. Later on, we read about his plans again, "When they asked him to stay for a longer period, he declined. But on taking leave of them he said, 'I will return to you if God wills, and he set sail from Ephesus" (Acts 18:20-21, ESV; see also 1 Corinthians 4:19).

We are called to realize that God is in control of everything, even the little things that we do not perceive. He is sovereign! Because of this, we should not boast of what we think we will do tomorrow. In a negative way, this is evil, as James points out. Every time we do not realize that God is in charge, we fail to give him glory.

Deo Volente! is the Latin for "God wills." This should be our attitude. It has never been forbidden to make plans; but when we do not recognize that anything we are going to do must be in line with God's will, our plans will not succeed. This is not a magical formula, it is a humbling submission to God's sovereign power and grace. The secret of our success is in God's hands; if he wills, not us. Adelaide A. Pollard wrote one of the most sublime words that we sing over the years:

> *Have Thine own way, Lord!*
> *Have Thine own way!*
> *Thou art the potter, I am the clay!*
> *Mold me and make me,*
> *After Thy will,*
> *While I am waiting,*
> *Yielded and still."*

The Word of God brings us comfort in knowing that when we trust in God, even the desires of our hearts will be blessed by him. "Trust in the LORD and do good; dwell in the land and enjoy safe pasture. Delight yourself in the LORD and he will give you the desires of your heart. Commit your way to the LORD; trust in him and he will do this" (Psalm 37:3-5).

Doing the Right Thing

The conclusion of chapter 4 brings us to the verse 17, "Therefore, the one who knows the right thing to do, and does not do it, to him it is sin" (NASV). James wants us to realize that in order to walk with the Lord, we must cling to this teaching from the Scripture. The right thing to do is not only to submit ourselves to his sovereign will, but also to walk in friendship with God, to walk in humility before him, and to walk in the holy fear of his judgment.

The entire teaching of Chapter 4 is here put as the right thing to do. This is a very important thing to keep in mind; but also to maintain us in check. For a number of years I have struggled with the meaning of this verse in the very end of this particular chapter. Somehow, it did not make much sense to me as tried to relate it to the previous passage we are now studying; and, indeed, it really does not make sense unless we take the entire chapter 4 into consideration. James is suggesting that, in view of what he is teaching now, we know what is the right thing to do.

We are called to do the right thing. Again, here we have the essence of the letter: do what the Word is teaching, walk the walk, do what you believe. Christianity is a very practical faith; if we fail in practicing it, then we commit sin. My father is over ninety years-old and he has never had an automobile in his entire life. Public transportation is very good in Brazil and he has used it for most of his days. I remember one day when he went downtown to run some errands. Upon his return he told us that while he was sitting comfortably, there was a pregnant woman standing by him. A lot of younger people were also sitting down, none of them offered their seats to the woman. My father did. Then I asked him why he did that. His answer was quite embarrassing for me to hear: "Well, son, the Apostle James wrote that if we know the right thing to do and we don't do it, in that we are committing a sin." I rested my case.

Chapter 14

Impatience Toward the Rich: The Test of Justice

James 5:1-6

I know that God has given us the use of goods, but only as far as is necessary. . . . It is absurd and disgraceful for one to live magnificently and luxuriously when so many are hungry (Clement of Alexandria, A.D. 150-215).

How far, O rich, do you extend your senseless avarice? Do you intend to be the sole inhabitants of the earth? Why do you drive out the fellow sharers of nature, and claim it all for yourselves? The earth was made for all, the rich and the poor, in common. Why do you rich men claim it as your exclusive right? . . . Property hath no rights. The earth is the Lord's, and we are his offspring (St. Ambrose, A.D. 340-397).

There is a great need for social concern and action in the Christian Church. At this point, James continues to draw his teaching in his letter from the teachings of Jesus Christ. Here we see how much he learned from the Lord. He remembers the teachings of the Sermon on the Mount, for example: "Blessed are those who hunger and thirst for righteousness, for they will be filled" (Matthew 5:6), but also the teachings on treasures in heaven (Matthew 6:19-24), how we should trust in the Lord for everything, not worrying about what to eat or what to dress (Matthew 6:25-32), and how to seek first the Kingdom of God and all its righteousness, knowing that everything else will be given to us (Matthew 6:33). He also leads us to the parables of the rich fool (Luke 12:13-21); of the prodigal son (Luke 15:11-32) and of the rich man and Lazarus (Luke 16:19-31). James is reaching his audience with a number of teachings of Jesus through this very uncomfortable passage.

Quoting from a source that I have in hands, I want to use the following illustration as an opening for this chapter: "Upton Sinclair once read this bit of James to a group of ministers after attributing it to Emma Goldman, an anarchist agitator. The ministers reacted with indignation against the effrontery of her diatribe and declared that she ought to be deported! (in Burton S. Easton and Gordon Poteat, *The Epistle of James, The Interpreter's Bible* 1957:12/62; citing Upton Sinclair, *The Profits of Religion* (Pasadena: Calif.: The Author, 1918: 287-290). I have the impression that if someone read this same passage and attributed it to a liberal politician or a community organizer of today, the reaction of many an evangelical would have been the same. The question that I keep raising through my ministry in the past number of years is whether we, as pastors, should preach on social justice from the pulpit or not. It is disconcerting to me to realize that we should, but with the necessary biblical wisdom for what we have to say, of course. The problem is that we pastors are afraid of not reaching out with the message. I believe that if we bring forth sound biblical messages, the church will experience great transformation in various areas. My main reason for that is the fact that Jesus Christ, by bringing his teaching of the Kingdom, taught profound lessons on social issues, not only for his day but for our days. Here we find James doing the same; and, as we will see ahead, when he speaks like an Old Testament prophet, he brings to us the reality of the ministry of those men who had been sent by the Lord to speak prophetic words no only to Israel but to the surrounding nations. I once heard one of my seminary professors say that Jesus is a very political person; I have to agree with his argument: "The first minute he mentioned the word 'kingdom,' he was already a political

The Wisdom Of James

figure." Adding to that, Jesus is the King of kings and Lord of lords; which is a clear political title for our Savior.

Again, let me formulate the question as we deal with this text and we must raise it with a humble and obedient attitude: Should we address social and political issues from the pulpit? This question leads to a number of other ones, all related to the social dimension of our Christian Faith. We Evangelicals have left this important arena of biblical teaching in the hands of the so-called "social gospelers" for a number of years. Fortunately, in the past twenty years or so, the Evangelical Church has raised to the challenge of the Gospel in favor of a more just world, providing a great deal of new information and sound biblical teaching on this issue.

We understand that a pastor should be theologically and biblically sound. He should preach from the wealth of biblical teachings that lead the Church of Jesus Christ to a complete understanding of the Gospel of the Kingdom of God. Therefore, the pastor who preaches so eloquently from Romans, for instance, should also preach from Amos, Jeremiah, Isaiah, Micah, and other prophets from the Old Testament. The Gospel of the Kingdom is both in Word and in Deed. It is Amos who brings a strong word of awakening to us on this important issue of Justice: "You who turn justice into bitterness and cast righteousness to the ground. . . . you hate the one who reproves in court and despise him who tells the truth, you trample on the poor and force him to give you grain. Therefore, though you have built stone mansions, you will not live in them; though you have planted lush vineyards, you will not drink their wine. For I know how many are your offenses and how great your sins" (Amos 5:7, 10-11a).

I would like to suggest that the theme for this text deals primarily with yet another important test in our Christian Faith. It also carries a serious warning to the rich people; this text will certainly deal with the rich believers, but also addresses those who are affluent yet without a saving faith in Jesus Christ. The test for the Church here is related with some major agendas of the Old Testament Prophets, the test of Justice. It is key, at this stage to observe that the "tone of voice" in James here resembles very closely the appeals that the prophets brought to Israel in so many occasions.

The Way of Wisdom Leads to Righteousness

"Now listen, you rich, weep and wail because of the misery that is coming upon you" (v. 1). The implications for this point come straight from the entire body of the Letter of James. His concern for the True Religion is around the wisdom that comes from heaven; therefore, the emphasis for the entire letter is surrounded by the voice of the Holy Spirit. Here James is again addressing his audience in a highly prophetic way. This reminds us of Isaiah 3:14-15, for example: "The LORD enters into judgment against the elders and leaders of his people: 'It is you who have ruined my vineyard; the plunder from the poor is in your houses. What do you mean by crushing my people and grinding the faces of the poor?' declares the Lord, the LORD Almighty." Also, Isaiah continues to bring forth more related prophetic words to God's people, "Woe to those who make unjust laws, to those who issue oppressive decrees, to deprive the poor of their rights and withhold justice from the oppressed of my people, making widows their prey and robbing the fatherless" (Isaiah 10:1-2). Back to Amos, we can also see that, "Hear this word, you cows of Bashan on Mount Samaria, you women who oppress the poor and crush the needy and say to your husbands, 'Bring us some drinks!'" (Amos 4:1). Micah voices the same concern by saying, "Woe to those who plan iniquity, to those who plot evil on their beds! At morning's light they carry it out because it is in their power to do it. They covet fields and seize them, and houses, and take them. They defraud a man of his home, a fellowman of his inheritance" (Micah 2:1-2). This is why James addresses his people as a prophet; speaking in a language that they will certainly listen and understand.

The key question at this point is: Who are the rich James is talking about? Initially I want to say that any person who lacks wisdom is going to fail in this important area of his or her life; they will fail miserably in how to deal with their wealth and what the Gospel demands for justice and righteousness in their new life with Jesus. In fact, Jesus has a word for those who are rich and have not changed their lives: "Woe to you who are rich, for you have already received your comfort. Woe to you who are well fed now, for you will go hungry. Woe to you who laugh now, for you will mourn and weep" (Luke 6:24-25).

The other question is about where are those rich people: Are they inside or outside the Church? Some scholars debate on this issue and suggest that James is talking to those who are oppressing the poor believers; we are reminded that the Church in the Diaspora was being persecuted when James wrote this letter. But one might ask, Why would James write to the Church and expect that unchurched people would read his letter? In fact, we know that there were many rich people in the early church. In a positive way, some of them were selling their properties and giving the money to the Apostles so they could help the poor (Acts 4:34-35); but, we should also think that there were many rich people who came to Jesus and were still living their former lives, in the way they had learned from long ago. I suggest that this was a visible and aching problem in the Church; otherwise, James would not have spent time to address it. He wanted to pass on the message from God that the Lord does not condone injustice in his Kingdom; much less in his Church.

Another way to see it is that James indeed was addressing the oppressing rich from outside. He had addressed the rich from within already in 1:9-11 and 2:1-7. Now, he may have the outsider in mind. We are reminded also that the Old Testament prophets have addressed the nations surrounding Israel with heavy words from the Lord (Isaiah, Jeremiah, Ezekiel, among others). This has to do with the understanding that the Lord is the Lord of all, and because of this he is also the Judge over all. The Book of Psalms is filled with passages that show God as the Judge over the nations. Here in James' case, he may be addressing those who probably would not even read this Epistle but he had another important reason for doing so: He wanted to show his brothers and sisters in Christ that there is hope for justice when the Lord Jesus returns. He mentions the "last days" and later, "the Lord's coming" (5:7). This message is linked with two important themes from the Prophets: the end of times (cf. Jeremiah 23:20; Ezekiel 38:16; Hosea 3:5; and Joel 2:28) and the final judgment of God (Deuteronomy 24:4; Isaiah 10:16-17; 30:27; Ezekiel 15:7, and Amos 5:6). The use of the "Lord Almighty," "Lord Sabaoth," or "Lord of hosts" demonstrates the weight of his admonition and the power of God as the Judge over the rich. Kistemaker puts it this way, "God the omnipotent is on the side of the downtrodden. He puts his majestic power to work to vindicate his people and to mete out swift justice to their adversaries."

Another audience becomes the center of attention of the Epistle, not necessarily of James in himself. If we believe that this Epistle is inspired by the Holy Spirit, all of its message applies to the Church throughout the years until the return of the Lord. Thus, we may see that the Epistle address the issue of wealth and affluence in the Church today. How many rich people in the Church today need to read this passage?

Here we see the impatience of James toward the rich. Although he speaks as an Old Testament prophet, he does not give them a chance for repentance in this passage. I agree with Calvin when he comments that, "They are mistaken, as I think, who consider that James here exhorts the rich to repentance." He adds, "It seems to me to be a simple denunciation of God's judgment, by which he meant to terrify them without giving them any hope of pardon; for all that he says tends only to despair."

Is this passage relevant to us today? Of course it is! Throughout Church History we see how the Church has grown rich over the centuries. The accumulation of wealth in the Church is something to think about. Time and time again, we are confronted with the uncomfortable situation we face towards the poor and downtrodden. This goes both corporately and individually. It permeates numerous branches of the Christian churches, and it does not respect barriers. The prophetic voice of James has a continuous effect throughout history and no church or Christian individual is immune to the danger of this sin.

Again, I think this pericope has a profound normative implication for the Church. The wisdom from above will certainly lead the Church to practice righteous acts of compassion towards the poor. It is the same wisdom that will turn the hearts of newly converted rich people to a new understanding of the values of the Kingdom and how they should treat those who are working for them, which is the case of Paul's concern when he wrote to the Colossians, "Masters, provide your slaves with what is right and fair, because you know that you also have a Master in heaven" (Colossians 4:1; see also Ephesians 6:9).

The Way of Injustice Leads to Judgment

There are four demonstrations of how the rich in the Early Church were reaching to the final confrontation with the Lord Almighty. As one commentator says, "one sin always leads to others." This is just an affirmation of what the Bible teaches over and over again. One abyss leads to another. The four interlinked sins in this passage are: hoarded wealth, theft through fraud, self-indulgence and judicial murder. It is our job to relate what was going on then to what we see happening today in our affluent society. It seems to me that there is no difference between then and now. I learned a lesson years ago that I often apply to life: "the names change, but the tendencies continue the same." Here is the same: throughout the centuries we continue to see the same tendencies in human hearts. It is a sad thing to realize, but that is the truth in every layer of society.

Hoarded Wealth

Before I go any further, I want to say that there is nothing particularly wrong with wealth. The Bible shows many of God's people who were considerably wealthy. Abraham, Joseph, David, Solomon, Joseph of Arimathea, and Barnabas. The problem with Solomon, however, is that he fell into the trap of his own thirst for possessions and power and ended up oppressing the people for more taxes. But, Proverbs 10:22 teaches us that, "The blessing of the LORD brings wealth, and he adds no trouble to it. We are reminded, nonetheless, that the *love of money* is the root of all evil (1 Timothy 6:10). We should keep in mind that wealth is given to us so we may serve our neighbors. Paul's concern with the rich is pictured this way, "Command those who are rich in this present world not to be arrogant nor to put their hope in wealth, which is so uncertain, but to put their hope in God, who richly provides us with everything for our enjoyment. Command them to be good, to be rich in good deeds, and to be generous and willing to share. In this way they will lay

The Wisdom Of James

up treasure for themselves as a firm foundation for the coming age, so that they may take hold of the life that is truly life" (1 Timothy 6:17-19).

The problem with wealth in this particular case is that the rich hoarded it and it started to show the results and proof against them in any court of law, mainly before the Court of the Lord. First, their wealth were being devoured in three different ways: "Your wealth has rotted, and moths have eaten your clothes. Your gold and silver are corroded" (vv. 2-3a). All the three verbs are in the perfect tense, suggesting that their wealth was in a continuous process of decay.

They had forgotten that God gives the provision of food in a cyclical way. What we have today, we will receive next year. This is the process of life. Kistemaker suggests that, "what God has provided in nature should be used for the daily sustenance of his creatures (Matt. 6:19). With proper distribution of these supplies no one needs to be hungry, for God's bountiful earth produces sufficient food for all." This implies that the accumulation of food for gain is a sin; it will rot and no one will eat from it. No wonder how much famine we find spread around the world! Because of greed, there is an immense source of food that is wasted away because it has not being properly distributed among the people, even within these United States. Tu Fu, an eighth-century Chinese poet, once wrote these lines, "Wine and meat are decaying in the palaces; While on the street are the corpses of those who have frozen to death." The other items are interrelated: Their stocked food was rotten, decayed; their garments were eaten by moths (see also, Job 13:28; Isaiah 51:8); their gold and silver, symbolizing their financial wealth, were corroded. Figuratively, this means that their wealth was nothing but worthless possessions. Putting this in the perspective of the last days, a commentator writes, "*the last days* have already begun and with them all earthly values have lost their meaning." Thus, the rich were accumulating the wrath of God upon themselves as they accumulated their riches without any concern for those who are in need.

There is a powerful development and application to all of this: They were building up their case against themselves. Because of their hoarding, they were going to be judged accordingly by fire. We see the similarity of James teaching with that of Jesus in showing them what kind of treasure they were accumulating. Their treasure was nothing but the accumulation of God's wrath against them in the last days; that is, in the Day of Judgment. Another reason to affirm that the intention of James is to show how God's justice will be served on those who oppress the poor. Pedrito Maynard-Reid has the following to say, "It is to the economically rich persons who oppress the poor that James offers no call to repentance, but only pronouncements of judgment."

Theft Through Fraud

"Look! The wages you failed to pay the workmen who mowed your fields are crying out against you. The cries of the harvesters have reached the ears of the Lord Almighty" (v. 4a). "The sin of greedily hoarding riches instead of sharing them with the poor prompts the sinner to rob the poor" (Kistemaker). Here, James brings the issue out in the open; the fields cannot hide the sins of the rich oppressors. "Here they can see the injustice poor people suffer at the hands of the rich."

"The wages you failed to pay." The Bible has always taught that the wages of the poor are to be paid by the end of the work's day (cf. Matthew 20:8). Leviticus 19:13 reads, "Do not defraud your neighbor or rob him. Do not hold back the wages of a hired man overnight." Sometimes, all the poor has to buy food for their families is that money they made in a single day. This is a common thing in many parts of the world, (but also in the United States). For many years, I have seen many hiring people to work in their homes; people who would not have food on their table unless they are paid at the end of that workday. There are the *diaristas* (daily workers in Portuguese) who work in cleaning, ironing, cooking, and so forth, for families in Brazil. Many of them go to the grocery store to buy the food for that evening and the next day just after they leave their daily job. Deuteronomy 24:14-15 reemphasizes the same principle, "Do not take advantage of a hired man who is poor and needy, whether he is a brother Israelite or an alien living in one of your towns. Pay him his wages each day before sunset, because he is poor and is counting on it. Otherwise he may cry to the LORD against you, and you will be guilty of sin."

The voice of the poor got God's attention. James uses a very powerful name for God in this passage, which demonstrates how serious this sin is. He says that "The cries of the harvesters have reached the ears of the Lord Almighty." Other translations render "The Lord Sabaoth." Peter Davids puts this comment in this way: "The term 'Lord Sabaoth' used here can only heighten this sense by referring to the majestic power of the prophetic God of Isaiah and the judgment which did follow his prophecy." This is the cry of the powerless poor of today as well. The worst kind of poverty is powerlessness; it is when the poor do not have any voice, nobody to claim their case. That's why the Lord listens to the cry of the powerless with great compassion; that's why his wrath is fiercer than we can even imagine.

Self-Indulgence

In this context, indulgence is strictly linked to the money that has been robbed from the poor. It is a sin to deprive the poor and live a extravagant lifestyle. There are numerous multinational corporations that exploit the poor around the world in order to make a profit; the worst part of it is the luxurious way they live and brag about their own success. This is the lifestyle that the rich man had and deprived Lazarus of having it (Luke 16:19). This is what the prodigal son did by squandering his wealth in wild living (Luke 15:13). But the Lord says through his Prophet James, "you have fattened yourselves in the day of slaughter."

This is a sobering admonition from the Lord. We live in such affluence and we seem to have forgotten that more than ninety percent of the world's population live in complete poverty. Some statistics show that the world is owned by about 520 families. There are a few billionaires who have enough money to buy a number of nations around the world. As a Christian nation, our country is guilty of the sin of self-indulgence and the cry of the poor who have been exploited by our giant corporations is getting to the ear of the Lord of Hosts.

The self-indulgence of the rich has called for the Day of Judgment upon them. They are fattened and ready for their own slaughter. Davids presents a number of passages that are related to that Day of Judgment. I want to just include some of those passages for your personal study at this moment: Psalms 22:29; 37:20; 49:14; Isaiah 30:33; 34:5-8; Jeremiah 46:10; 50:26-27; Lamentations 2:21-22; Ezekiel 39:17; Revelation 19:17-21.

Judicial Murder

"You have condemned and murdered innocent men, who were not opposing you" (v.6) By taking them to court (James 2:6), the rich people "directly or indirectly. . . . killed a human being who was unable to defend himself" (Kistemaker). Joshua ben Sira voices the same idea, "The bread of the needy is the life of the poor; whoever deprives them of it is a man of blood. To take away a neighbor's living is to murder him; to deprive an employee of his wages is to shed his blood" (Sir. 34:21-22, RSV).

The two terms *condemn* and *murder* equal to the clear subversion of justice by using their wealth. This is how the ungodly, the wicked people say about the inconvenience of the poor: "Let us oppress the righteous poor man. . . . Let us lie in wait for the righteous man, because he is inconvenient to us and opposes our actions; he reproaches us for sins against the law" (Wis. 2:10, 12, RSV). This reminds me of my home church in Brazil. In the year of 1965, a new pastor came to serve our church and he started to preach about the needs of the poor and downtrodden. His message was centered in the Gospel but brought the bitterness of condemnation to the minority of the rich people in charge of the church. In about two years, that small group led the pastor away, he and his family. This also reminds me of Chico Mendes, a poor logger in the State of Acre, Brazil. He started a movement against the powerful corporations and other individuals who were destroying a great part of the Amazon; soon later he was mercilessly killed by a hit man. Mendes became the symbol of contemporary heroism and martyrdom in my home country. Not long ago, an American nun was killed in the Pará State, Brazil, because she was, for a number of years, helping the

The Wisdom Of James

poor and providing means of justice for those who were voiceless. The list would certainly be too long to mention at this point.

We may see this act of cowardice as both "symbolic" or "spiritualized" murder and physical murder. It is somewhat difficult to see it as a real act of murdering someone, but history will continue to show that this is the case. Maynard-Reid presses toward the physical murder and among his arguments he quotes Thomas Hanks, as he wrote about "Why People Are Poor." In his writing he has this to add,

> *It is fascinating, though profoundly disturbing, to see the conservative evangelical mentality at work to make James more palatable. In James 4, in a description of class struggle ("wars," "fights," "ye fight," "ye war," verses 1-2) motivated by greed ("ye covet," verse 2), and expressing itself in all manner of capitalist initiatives ("we will trade and we will make a profit," verse 2b). "Murder?" say the commentators. "Impossible, free enterprise, capitalist ingenuity, the American way of life, an honest buck; what's good for General Motors is good for the country." But James says "you murder." The mechanisms of oppression deprive the poor of their land and other means of livelihood and leave them without the essentials for life (1 Kings 21; Luke 16:19-31).*

We think that those social concerns are new. Because of the Social Gospel movement, our Evangelical heritage has been damaged and we think that it is not biblical to pursue Justice and Righteousness. This is not true; we, as children of God, as citizens of the Kingdom of God, are the ones who should go out to the streets and proclaim that there is hope and justice in the message of the Gospel. We should join brothers in Christ like Clement of Alexandria (150-215) who had the courage to raise his voice against the injustices of his time, which are no different from ours. This is how he voiced his concerns, "I know that God has given us the use of goods, but only as far as necessary. . . . It is absurd and disgraceful for one to live magnificently and luxuriously when so many are hungry." Another

The Wisdom Of James

brother, St. Ambrose (340-397) brought these words to the fore, "How far, O rich, do you extend your senseless avarice? Do you intend to be the sole inhabitants of the earth? Why do you drive out the fellow sharers of nature, and claim it all for yourselves. The earth was made for all, the rich and poor, in common. Why do you rich men claim it as your exclusive right? . . . Property hath no rights. The earth is the Lord's, and we are his offspring" (Quoted in Upton Sinclair, *The Cry for Justice* [Philadelphia, PA: John C. Winston, 1915:397]).

As we continue to seek God's will for our lives; let us be reminded of the Justice of his Kingdom. We are heirs of his Righteousness; in Christ Jesus we are redeemed for his Glory. We are also called to "reign with him." Therefore, we have a lot to learn on how to live our lives under the wisdom that comes from heaven. As I mentioned in the opening of this chapter, there is nothing intrinsically wrong with being rich. The wrong side of it is when the rich do not live their lives under the guidance of the Lord's teaching. This is the center of James concern in his letter.

Chapter 15

Waiting for Deliverance: The Test of Patience

James 5:7-12

James deals with the Second Coming of Jesus Christ in a very simple yet powerful way. He talks about it as a Classic Old Testament Prophet, but also in the same way the Lord Jesus spoke in his teaching while among us. He does not discuss the complexities of the eschatological meaning of his coming; rather, he deals with the return of Jesus Christ as the Day of Judgment, and also as an imminent event; again, in the same fashion of our Master and Lord. Here, he mentions twice that day, and in the previous passage, when he was addressing the rich, he also made mention of the fact that they, the rich, had "hoarded wealth in the last days," and that they had "fattened [themselves] in the day of slaughter."

Now, he addresses the issue of patience and perseverance once more. This time as it is linked with the oppression that came upon the poor ones. The center of the message at this point is related to the urgent need for his brothers and sisters to let it go; that is, to let the Lord take care of those matters that were causing them pain and suffering. Even though they are commanded to be patient under their present oppressive situation, their patience should not be the same as a blunt and passive acceptance of what was going. They were not to succumb to any fatalistic idea of life; no "*que sera*

sera" passivity was allowed. Rather, they were commanded to leave matters in the hands of the Lord, because he was taking care of all of them, as we find in the following passages: "It is mine to avenge; I will repay. In due time their foot will slip; their day of disaster is near and their doom rushes upon them" (Deuteronomy 32:35; cf. Romans 12:19). Again, "For we know him who said, 'It is mine to avenge; I will repay,' and again, 'The Lord will judge his people'" (Hebrews 10:30; cf. Deuteronomy 32:36; Psalm 135:14).

This chapter seeks to find an affirmative motivation for all of us who patiently persevere in the faith, even if we are undergoing hardships. The glorious return of the Lord Jesus is the key for our persistence in waiting for that great day of final redemption; that's why we should patiently wait for our final deliverance.

The Lord is coming soon; therefore, we must be patient and wait for his great and final redemption. In fact, there is an intrinsic relationship between our daily walk with the Lord and our expectancy of his return. Elsewhere we are admonished to walk as if the Lord would arrive at any minute; thus, we must be prepared for that glorious day. The illustration given by Jesus in the parable of the Ten Virgins is powerful (Matthew 25:1-13). Paul reminds us to owe nothing but love and to be prepared for the day of the Lord, "The night is nearly over; the day is almost here. So let us put aside the deeds of darkness and put on the armor of light. Let us behave decently, as in the daytime, not in orgies and drunkenness, not in sexual immorality and debauchery, not in dissension and jealousy. Rather, clothe yourselves with the Lord Jesus Christ, and do not think about how to gratify the desires of the sinful nature" (Romans 13:12-14). Peter, writing to the believers in the Diaspora, reminds us of the same thing, "But the day of the Lord will come like a thief. . . . Since everything will be destroyed in this way, what kind of people ought you to be? You ought to live holy and godly lives as you look forward to the day of God and speed its coming. . . . So then, dear friends, since you are looking forward to this, make every effort to be found spotless, blameless and at peace with him" (2 Peter 3:10a, 11, 14). The passage we are dealing with now is highly eschatological; that is, it deals with the end of times and how we should be prepared for it.

A commentator suggests also that this passage, although it is linked to the preceding with the adverb "therefore," covers a more general aspect of James' intent. He suggests that "the following exhortation is quite general; patience under any form of hardship or distress is enjoined, not merely under oppression by the rich. As the end of the world is at hand and the righteous will soon receive their reward, they can disregard their present troubles and wait patiently with sure confidence." As we will see below, such approach is plausible, but I believe the intent of James is to bring comfort for those who are oppressed and voiceless because of the persecution they were receiving from the rich people. Here, James wants to bring hope for justice to them; therefore, the link with the preceding section is stronger than to the general corpus of the Epistle.

Wait in Patience for the Deliverance of the Lord

It is difficult to hold your peace when you are under some kind of oppression. James, knowing that for a fact, tries to encourage his brothers and sisters during their moment of trial, in that case, the oppressive treatment they were receiving from the rich people. "Therefore," he says, "be patient, brothers, until the Lord's coming." It is in times like these that we are called to persevere in our integrity of life as Christians.

Kistemaker points out that, "Patience is a virtue possessed by few and sought by many." He goes on by saying that, "Patience is the art of enduring someone whose conduct is incompatible with that of others and sometimes even oppressive." J. B. Lightfoot defines Patience as "the self-restraint which does not hastily retaliate a wrong." (In dealing with God's patience, Louis Berkhof defines it as, "that aspect of the goodness or love of God in virtue of which He bears with the forward and evil in spite of their long continued disobedience.") This is very true! The most difficult thing for us to do is to quiet down when we are under persecution or in any oppressive situation. Here we find the brother of our Lord Jesus telling his congregation to endure patiently the oppression that is coming upon them in several ways. We should remember that he is writing like a Hebrew prophet; he is consistent in his line of thought throughout

177

his letter, "Consider it pure joy, my brothers, whenever you face trials of many kinds." He is calling his readers to endure those trials in patience. This particular passage is more intentional than generalized, however. He uses the adverb "then" to link this pericope to the preceding one; clearly naming the kind of trial they were going through: oppression by the rich people against their churches spread in the Diaspora.

He uses the simplest way of describing how they should exercise patience. The example that he introduces is that of the farmer who patiently waits for the land to yield its valuable crop. He patiently waits for the rains in October (James is dealing with this issue based on his knowledge of the timing in Palestine) and then in early April. There is nothing they can do but wait for the land to go through its cycle. After they sow their grain seed, they patiently wait for the right time of harvesting.

In this instance, James reiterates that the time of waiting is the most important reason in their lives: the return of the Lord Jesus Christ. He is near! He is coming soon! The Word of God cannot fail them, it cannot fail us! He brings forth for the second time the return of Jesus so that everyone will be comforted by such a great promise of the Lord. It is key to notice that James is calling the reader to do the same, but mostly in "establishing their hearts," according to Douglas Moo. It is here that we must pay attention to what James is trying to convey to his readers: as they exercised patience, their hearts were growing stronger and ready to have their encounter with the Lord Jesus Christ. "Stand firm," keep your hearts strong, do not loose heart; the need to maintain our faith in the promises of the Lord is here vindicated. When James shows the nearness of the coming of the Lord, he wanted to inform them (and us today) that the Lord is at the door. Again, we must be prepared for that day. In a similar way, Paul addressed the same issue when he wrote to the Thessalonians, "May he strengthen your hearts so that you will be blameless and holy in the presence of our God and Father when our Lord Jesus comes with all his holy ones" (1 Thessalonians 3:13). Again, "May our Lord Jesus Christ himself and God our Father, who loved us and by his grace gave us eternal encouragement and good hope, encourage your hearts and strengthen you in every good deed and word" (2 Thessalonians 2:16-17). Another reminder, "while we wait for the blessed hope—the glorious appearing of our great God and Savior, Jesus Christ" (Titus 2:13).

Stop Grumbling Against Each Other

The second admonition in this passage is that they should not grumble against each other. This is probably one problem they were facing in the church; brothers and sisters were impatient with each other. Perhaps blaming each other, quarrelling and fighting, and misusing their words (ch. 3:1-12; 5:12). Such thing should not happen; we are called to live in peace and respecting each other, which is the fulfillment of the Law of Love, the Law of Christ (2:1-12). This is the way of the Lord, the way of wisdom, "But the wisdom that comes from heaven is first of all pure; then peace-loving, considerate, submissive, full of mercy and good fruit, impartial and sincere. Peacemakers who sow in peace raise a harvest of righteousness" (3:17-18). Proverbs has an important word on this matter, "A hot-tempered man stirs up dissention, but a patient man calms a quarrel" (Proverbs 15:18). Also, "Better a patient man than a warrior, a man who controls his temper than one who takes a city" (Proverbs 16:32).

By grumbling against each other, the members of the church were placing their judgment on those who had nothing to do with their misfortune. James' concern at this point is that his people should not project their own frustrations against their own peers; they all were being persecuted. The ones who were oppressing them were not there to hear any of those words of accusation against them. Instead, they should try to bring healing among themselves; not quarreling or fights.

We have a lot to learn from this passage. We live in a society that is characterized by its ability to cast blame on everyone else. We are quick to blame one another for anything that happens to us; because of this we are unable to handle our lives in responsible ways. Just *Blame it to Rio*, some would suggest. The problem is that we forget that we will be judged according to the measure by which we judge others. Again, we find a close relationship of this teaching

The Wisdom Of James

with the teaching of Jesus Christ (cf. Matthew 7:1-5). Every time a person casts a blameful judgment on each other, a new wound is exposed.

Instead, the people of the church should join hands and wait for the righteous judgment of the Lord: "The Judge is standing at the door!" Here we see the eschatological dimension of the last day. Again, James is reminding his readers of the coming of the Lord, this time as the Judge over all.

Follow the Examples of Other Brethren

James draws the attention of his readers to some important examples. But before I continue, I want to pause to explain the word "example" in James writing. This is a powerful way of addressing the issue that he is dealing with. The word "example" is an emphatic one; it appears in the very beginning of the sentence. James wants to direct his readers attention to some examples that are key in the lives of all of them; those are concrete examples of endurance and perseverance, and his church members knew them well.

He talks of the prophets who went before them. Perhaps the first prophet that God used in Scripture is Noah, who spoke in the name of the Lord for more than a hundred years, and persisted in building an ark that literally didn't make much sense even to him. He had no knowledge of what rain was until it came down; but he persisted in preaching the gospel to his people. Elijah is another example of patience and perseverance. One cannot leave Jeremiah out of this important list of patient prophets; a man who apparently did not see much—or almost nothing—results of his ministry. Other prophets come to mind, among them Daniel, Isaiah, and Ezekiel.

But James devotes time to talk about Job. James does not talk about Job's patience here. In fact, Job was not very patient in at least two occasions: when he cursed the day he was born and when he complained about the long speeches of his three friends. But who else in the Bible shows more clearly the virtue of perseverance than this man of God? As we read in the beginning of the Epistle, "faith develops perseverance" (1:3), but only after we face trials and temptations. As a commentator puts it, "In vs. 11 **the steadfastness of**

The Wisdom Of James

Job (RSV; cf. on 1:3) is much better than the **patience of Job** (KJV), which has become a traditional phrase in English; for while Job was constantly steadfast in his moral integrity, his protests against his sufferings can scarcely be described as 'patient.'"

Job was a man just like you and me; but he persevered in his faith. Although he went through incredible pain and tribulation, although he was lacking in patience a couple of times (at least as recorded in the book), he persevered in believing that the Lord was with him all the time. Some scholars question James' use of this example of Job, but I think the point he wants to make is based on Job's persever-ance and "what the Lord finally brought about." Here we see the outcome, the result of Job's endurance—another way of interpreting patience. The outcome of his faithfulness under tremendous trial is shown in the very end of the book of Job. James made the comment on his life, "You have heard of Job's perseverance and have seen what the Lord finally brought about." The most commendable word about Job is that he did not sin against God through any word that he said. The result of his faith and perseverance is wonderfully demon-strated in the last chapter of the Book of Job, "The LORD blessed the latter part of Job's life more than the first" (Job 42:12a).

We live by examples. We should follow the examples of people who are godly and wise. There are many who fit that category in our lives: a teacher, a classmate, a father, a mother, a brother, a sister. The list grows as we look around; the Lord puts people in our lives to inspire and motivate us to overcome our times of trials and temptations.

Be Truthful in What You Say

James is still talking about the brevity of life and the nearness of the day of the Lord when he draws this important teaching from the Sermon on the Mount. Again, he takes almost word by word of what Jesus taught about oaths in his majestic Sermon (cf. Matthew 5:34-37). Some scholars suggest that this verse has little to do with the preceding ones, and that it is a continuation of his teaching about the usage of our tongue. There is a link with that passage, of course, but I do not seem to understand why he would bring forth this argument after such a long list of other admonitions. The best way to see it through this perspective, however, is to affirm again that James is dealing with true religion and the wisdom that comes from heaven. In that sense, granted!

But I see it as an example of the way we should live our lives in face of the second coming of Jesus. Peter, for example, teaches in his second letter that we should live holy lives and be ready for the day of the Lord (2 Peter 3:10-12). Here, I would like to suggest that James is calling us to the realization that every single word that comes out of our mouth will be counted in the day of the Lord. That is clear in Jesus Christ's teachings, but here the issue has more to do with two important areas that are included in this passage: First, the issue of oppression that James talks in the beginning of chapter 5. If they were called to a place of judgment against the rich, their word must be "yes" or "no," but said in truth. This is significant because even when people are in an oppressive situation they should not change the truth for their own gain. We live in a society that is motivated by the possibility of suing others. As an example, as soon as one is involved in any kind of situation, he or she is already "educated" through the lenses of a victim; that is, as soon as we have anything done against us, it is our "prerogative" to act as victims, and thus to take the other part to court. The problem is that sometimes we may feel the urge of twist the truth a little in order to make more money out of that situation. We must remember always that the Lord is near and that he is the Judge above all.

The second aspect of this problem is that we are prone to blame our brothers and sisters for what might be happening to us in the church. That is why James commands us not to grumble against each other. Here we come to the problem of unreal expectations, for example. Sometimes what we may expect to happen to us is only in our heads and hearts, but the reality might be another very different from what we perceive it to be. We are unable to know the entire truth around us; be it a metaphysical one, or just any other reality that surrounds us experientially. Paul is quite correct when he deals with this important issue in 1 Corinthians, "For we know in part and we prophesy in part, but when perfection comes, the imperfect disappears. . . . Now we see but a poor reflection as in a mirror;

The Wisdom Of James

then we shall see face to face. Now I know in part; then I shall know fully, even as I am fully know" (1 Corinthians 13:9, 12). The lesson to learn here is that we must measure our words and speak the truth as it is; the way we are allowed to see it by the grace of God. Anything that exceeds or lacks in our given words will be counted before the Lord in his Glorious Day.

The Day of the Lord is at hand! It could happen at any moment, we must be prepared. Paul writes about it to the Church in Thessalonica, "All this is evidence that God's judgment is right, and as a result you will be counted worthy of the kingdom of God, for which you are suffering. God is just: He will pay back trouble to those who trouble you and give relief to you who are troubled, and to us as well. This will happen when the Lord Jesus is revealed from heaven in blazing fire with his powerful angels" (2 Thessalonians 1:5-7). The Author of Hebrews also speaks about that glorious day, "Just as man is destined to die once, and after that to face judgment, so Christ was sacrificed once to take away the sins of many people; and he will appear a second time, not to bear sin, but to bring salvation to those who are waiting for him" (Hebrews 9:27-28).

Because of this, we wait for the Great Day of Deliverance! We are called to patiently wait for that Glorious Day of Deliverance because he is coming soon! Maranatha! Come soon Lord Jesus!

Chapter 16

Earnest Prayer: The Test of Mutuality

James 5:13-18

These well-known verses are among the most neglected and misunderstood in the church today. First, they are neglected. When someone is in trouble, he readily prays. But when someone is happy, we do not hear him sing songs of praise. Our technological age has taken over and we have become a society that listens, not a people that sings. Another point. Although pastors make regular hospital calls to visit the sick, the practice of calling the elders of the church to pray over the sick seems to belong to a bygone age. One of the tasks of the elders in the church is to pray for the sick when they are called to do so; nevertheless, this work is usually assigned to the pastor. (Simon Kistemaker)

The more I think about prayer in this context, the more I see its relationship with our need to be transparent to each other. I see that the text shows how much we need each other. This passage is significant in many ways: first, it shows how much we need to persist in prayer, it is the effect of being patient in times of trouble; it is the means we have to communicate with God and also among ourselves about our struggles and needs. Secondly, it carries in itself a great sociological implication because it has an important ground of dependency on each other, beginning with the leadership of the Church.

Although I will touch base on the importance and power of prayer, I hope to accomplish another goal by dealing with our personal need to be transparent and to expect healing by doing so. Of course, prayer is the key element in this passage, but little will we accomplish unless we do understand why James is dealing with it in relation to the whole of the community.

Prayer is a community issue; the Church of Christ must understand that she will not survive unless there is serious public involvement in prayer; by that I mean *serious prayer*. Again, I think this is yet another test in our faith: the test of being transparent through times of need; the test of transparency through the healing ministry of prayer.

Another aspect of prayer in the church is the great necessity of compassion that accompanies the needs of the people. Not only must we be transparent to each other, we must have compassion for each other. I believe that the Church has a great need of prayer, but most of all, a need for compassionate prayer. I have experienced the presence of this kind of prayer in the church my wife and I attend. There is a significant movement of prayer going on there; as a result, I have seen a number of outcomes that I thought impossible to see under normal circumstances. The Lewis-Clark Valley, our "neck of the woods" here in Idaho, has been the center of a tremendous prayer movement in the past few years. There is a clear expectancy for a revival in our area; we have been praying for the land to be healed, for the conversion of the Native Americans who live in our area. We have been praying for a new missionary vision that will reach the ends of the earth. Slowly, but steadily, we start to see a number of brothers and sisters leaving for different mission fields. At the time of this writing, I am training a couple in preparation for mission somewhere in Asia, in a place of difficult access. We are going through the book of Acts together at the request of their mission organization; more than ever, we are convinced that without prayer there will be no mission work to be done under the precepts of the Kingdom of God.

I cover this chapter through two specific pair of lenses. First, I dealt with our need to be transparent with each other and then I tried to see the faith implications for our ministry and for our Christian life today. My goal, however, is to see prayer as the most important instrument of God to keep the Church together, as the glue that bind us together as the people of God.

Bottom Line Questions

Our brother James is a master when it comes to the down-to-the-point questions. His short, but direct questions bring in themselves a deep sense of urgency and also a commitment to more explorations on the subjects they cover. Here we see that he is dealing with important aspects of our Christian life. It is easy to point out the areas he is covering: troubles, happiness, sickness, broken relationships, and above all, the lack of faith when we pray. The latter statement is made clear by his emphasis that "prayer offered in faith will make the person well." Also, by giving the example of Elijah, he is making sure that the core of prayer is faith.

James does not go around the issue; he is direct to the point. His series of questions are clearly aimed to the real needs of the members of his church. He asks short questions, and provides short directives to those problems: "Is any one of you in trouble? He should pray. Is anyone happy? Let him sing songs of praise. Is any one of you sick? He should call the elders of the church to pray over him and anoint him with oil in the name of the Lord."

He is concerned with two major issues: troubles (hardships, afflictions, suffering) and sickness. These are the most common reasons for problems in the Church. When someone is facing troubles or is sick, it affects the entire body of Christ. If we are to consider the Church a Living Building, built with living stones (1 Peter 4-5), we are affected by the suffering of those who surround us, because we are part of the same body. It is interesting to observe that sometimes a small scratch disrupts the entire function of our bodies.

A member of our congregation had a long fight with cancer. She went to be with the Lord after that prolonged time when she fought a courageous battle which left a vacuum in our midst. During that time, the entire church remained together in prayer. Her suffering and death had a profound impact upon most of us. But the testimony of commitment in prayer brought a large segment of the church together. We continue to see the results of her testimony among ourselves and we know that her life was a source of inspiration for many.

We must learn from this passage that we need to go to the bottom line; to the real problems and suffering we are going through. It is imperative that we go beyond the denial of our problems and face them with courage; naming them by name. But also, having a clear assessment of what may be the cause of them. James brings this important lesson to us: realize that you have a problem as soon as you have the problem. As we do so, we cannot reside in a state of despair; rather, we must embrace our needs with faith and act in compassion for each other.

Be Transparent With Your Needs

The "bottom line questions" that we should ask will give us the clear understanding of our personal and corporate needs. Before we go to the Lord in prayer, it is elementary that we realize what is going on in our lives. Sometimes we do not know exactly what to pray (Romans 8:26) and then we must be aware that the Holy Spirit will assist us in doing so. But we know what our needs are when we search our hearts and also when we identify what is going on in our surroundings; that is, with our immediate needs. It has been my personal practice to ask the Lord for guidance on what I really need. A good outline for my exploration is taken from the Lord's Prayer but also I go to the Book of Psalms quite often in order to get to know my needs. It seems to me that the Psalmists, mostly David for that matter, express the feelings that I have about myself and how much I need the Lord on a daily basis. A portion of Scripture that helps me to be transparent with the Lord is the following, "Search me, O God, and know my heart; test me and know my anxious thoughts. See if there is any offensive way in me, and lead me in the way everlasting" (Psalm 139:23-24). Of course, the entire Psalm 139 is a demonstration that God knows me better than myself.

Times of Trouble

The first question raised by James is the prelude for a wonderful response of faith: "Is any one of you in trouble?" Here he is talking about the many troubles that his brothers and sisters were going through, but also he speaks to us today. Among the many troubles, we may list the following: *Persecutions* (James 5:1-5, 10); *Suffering* or *external misfortunes* (e.g.: Job, James 5:11); *Slander* (James 3:1-12; 2:6-7), and many other kinds of suffering that are external attacks against the children of God.

It is here that we come to the Lord in prayer. The brother of Jesus admonishes us: "He should pray." Our prayers are powerful to help us overcome such misfortunes; it is when we go to the Lord on our knees that he pours down the comfort of his Holy Spirit upon us. This is the response to our deepest needs. When we are in trouble, we should pray. The Lord knows what trouble we are in. He is the Lord of our lives and he is pleased to hear from us what is going on. This is the first area of our transparency: we must be transparent with God in the first place. We must realize that we have access to his Throne of Grace at any time through Jesus Christ, our Only Mediator (1 Timothy 2:5; Hebrews 10:19-23). The Lord says in Psalm 50:15, "and call upon me in the day of trouble; I will deliver you, and you will honor me." I am often reminded of the old song, "Nobody knows the trouble I've seen; nobody knows my sorrow; nobody knows the trouble I've seen…"

This great opportunity of prayer is taught all over the Bible. But I'd like to call just another follower of Jesus at this moment to help us better understand its importance: Paul, the Apostle to the Gentiles, calls us to never stop praying, because when we pray we receive the powerful blessings that the Lord has for us (cf. 1 Thessalonians 5:17-18). But one passage that really speaks to my heart is from Philippians, "Do not be anxious about anything, but in everything, by prayer and petition, with thanksgiving, present your requests to God. And the peace of God, which transcends all understanding, will guard your hearts and your minds in Christ Jesus" (Philippians 4:6-7).

Times of Joy

I grew up in a religious tradition that basically tries to hide any happiness. Actually, it seemed to me that anything religious should be as reverent as possible. By that, of course, you were not supposed to laugh; which is pretty hard in a culture like the one God planned to have me born into. Simply put, I grew up with the impression that to be a Presbyterian was equal to be really boring. Long sermons, even longer hymns that made no sense to me, I remember having absolutely no fun going to church. No wonder when I turned twelve, I left the church and embraced the world with all my heart! It was that pious façade that was part of the ritual that did not appeal to me.

I came to know Jesus Christ as my Lord and Savior much later at the age of twenty-two. During those days I was completely immersed in the occult, following an African-Brazilian religion, dealing with black magic, Spiritism, and so forth. I had my personal encounter with the Lord when I was on my way to a voodoo service in the crossroads in a nearby forest. There was no Billy Graham there for me; I was found alone by the Lord Jesus and as far as I remember, I even did not know what was happening with me until later, after I returned to the church.

Talking about boredom, I returned to the Presbyterian Church because it was the only place I felt safe then. But a new thing had invaded my heart: a tremendous joy that I had no words to explain. Life was no longer a confusing and threatening thing for me; I had a new smile on my face. The desire of praising the Lord came to me in a way I had never experienced before. All I could see was the light of blessings shedding upon my soul, within my heart. From then on, worshiping the Lord had a complete different meaning for me, even within a Presbyterian environment.

It is a fact in my life that I have struggled with a number of obstacles, trials, temptations and ailments ever since. The enemy of Jesus Christ is a fierce enemy of ours as well. There has been times in my life that I really thought I would not make it the next day. But that joy is still there. When I contemplate the glorious return of our Lord Jesus, I have the presence of that great joy in my heart. I am

The Wisdom Of James

always reminded of the words of Paul, "Rejoice in the Lord always. I will say it again: Rejoice!. . . The Lord is near" (Philippians 4:4-5).

This brief testimony leads me to the next part of James teaching. The result of prayer is clear: "Is anyone happy? Let him sing songs of praise." The Bible speaks about happiness and we seem not to pay much attention to it. Among several passages, we may look into the following: 1 Corinthians 14:15; Ephesians 5:19; Colossians 3:16, and Philippians 4:4-5. But one thing is true: the joy that comes after we receive a special touch of God generates songs in our hearts. That is why we are always reminded to rejoice in the Lord with hymns, psalms and spiritual songs. Those who have the impact of an answered prayer will sing to the Lord. Most of the thanksgiving prayers in the Bible are Psalms, just take the prayers of Miriam, Moses, David, Hannah and Job as examples. A praying person is also a singing person. Remember, James is talking to a person, not to many persons here. Singing is an important part of our personal worship to him. Sometimes we thank the Lord best with our voices in singing praises to him; more than during quiet moments of silent prayer. Our Lord is pleased to hear our singing; he enjoys the sound of our voices when they are filled with thanksgiving. Paul helps us with an important reminder that we ought to be thankful always but also that we should be a happy company of believers (cf. 1 Thessalonians 5:16-18).

Times of Sickness

There are times when the person goes through a different type of hardship: sickness. It is a time when that person seems to get lost in a maze of pain and personal disorientation. In such time, nothing seems to be in order; the person's time is taken from his hands completely, the focus for life seems to vanish away. A time of sickness brings other ailments that will magnify its corrosive effects on him. Loneliness and self-pity linger and depression is not far away. Day after day, he will call upon the Lord but answers are vague or no answers at all. This is the time when he needs to call the elders of the church and hope for their comfort in prayer.

The elders' involvement in this ministry is crucial for the overall needs of the person in need: Spiritually, Psychologically, and Physically. They are there as the overseers over that person's most crucial need at the moment. This is not a time to consider whether the gift of healing is implied. There is absolutely nothing in this passage that suggests that it is the exercise of the gift of healing. It is a command from the Lord in the normal occurrences of shepherding of the flock. The anointing with oil is symbolic of the power of the Holy Spirit, but the main focus of the text is on the prayer, not on the oil. The prayer is to be offered in faith; that is, the elders' faith is critical at this point. They will pray *"in the name of the Lord."* The text says that *"the Lord will raise him up."* That is, the text is here talking about a "clearly physical healing."

There is also an important part to consider in this text: The confession of sins is related to the process of healing. In this case, it is a personal, individual case; that is why the elders are there with the person. There are some sins that do not need to become public, but the elders are there to hear them on a private way. One important note at this point: Not all sickness is related to sin (e.g.: the blind man and Job). But there are sins that are intrinsically linked with some illnesses. That is why James uses the conditional clause: *"If he has sinned..."* Kistemaker adds an important note to the better understanding of this particular passage, "The statement 'if he has sinned, he will be forgiven' emphasizes the interrelatedness of body and soul. For instance, Jesus healed the paralytic spiritually when he said, 'Your sins are forgiven,' and physically by saying, 'Get up, take your mat and go home' (Mark 2:5, -11). Jesus heals soul and body to make man complete."

"He should call the elders of the church" — It is important for us to realize that James is telling the sick person to call the elders, not vice-versa. Sometimes we have the hard office of being an elder or a pastor, for that matter, because there is often that assumption that elders and pastors know who is sick and who is not sick in the Church. There are many members of the Church that are hurt because the pastor or the elders did not go to their homes, hospitals or nursing homes for a visit when they most needed them. I speak as a pastor at this moment: It is simply frustrating to learn that someone from the congregation *was* in the hospital a week ago. Usually the news come with that dosage of chastisement that it deserves: the pastor did not go there to visit brother John. Another aspect of this passage that needs to be emphasized is that the elders are expected to be the ones visiting those who are sick. I was once interviewed for a position in a particular church and the committee members asked me why I did not mark "visitation" as part of my qualifications (out of approximately thirty-five options, I could mark only twelve). I told them that I usually visit the sick upon request and that that part of the job description is more in line with the job description of the elders of the church. They seemed surprised by my answer and I had the opportunity to educate them later on this biblical principle; after I received the call to be their pastor, of course.

This is an important aspect of being transparent. We live in a society that has taught us not to share our weaknesses with anybody. We must put on a face, even when we cannot afford the pain in our hearts, in our souls, in our bodies. By calling the elders of the Church, that sick person is opening up his or her heart to the real need that is afflicting her or him. There is a significant dynamic going on when a person calls the elders to pray for her or him. The opportunity of being transparent brings forth the opportunity for healing but also for forgiveness of sins. I have the impression that the forgiveness implied here and in the next verse is related to the person's sins against other persons. It is an opportunity to rebuild broken relationships. I think that the text does not authorize any elder to proclaim forgiveness at the same level that God will forgive a person; this is more of a relational, social sin that may have taken place. Sometimes a person, after confessing his or her sins to God, must make restitution to others and that implies asking for forgiveness in front of others. True Salvation brings forth that disposition to a repentant heart, which was the case of Zacchaeus (Luke 19:1-10).

We Are Not Alone

"Confess your sins to each other and pray for each other" — This is the crux of the teaching of James in the passage. We should share our burdens with each other. In many cases, sickness is due to some hidden sin that has not been confessed. There is nothing in this passage that suggests that we should confess our sins to someone in private, like we see in the Roman Church. Also, this is a command that is mutual, not unilateral. Therefore, I am confident in suggesting that James is here talking about sins that are publicly affecting other persons or the community. In this case, if we need to confess our sins to someone whom we have sinned against, we should do it and pray with that person. If the sin is more public than that, it should be confessed in a situation where there will be a time for prayer and forgiveness. "So that you may be healed" is the result of confession and prayer, the person who is sick because of sin, will receive the healing that she or he needs. There is a therapeutic effect in doing so. Douglas Moo has a word about our mutuality in this aspect, "Mutual confession of sins, which James encourages as a habitual practice (this is suggested by the present tense of the imperative), is greatly beneficial to the spiritual vitality of a church."

Before I go any further, it is necessary to say that we are not alone in this situation. There are so many people who are sick because of their overwhelming problems, one of the symptoms of that is depression. Psalm 42 is a classic example of someone who is suffering from depression because of the overwhelming load upon him. Psalms 32, 38, 51, among many, are examples of someone (King David, in those cases) who was sick because of his sins. John Calvin points out that, ". . . we indeed see that David, when afflicted with disease and seeking relief, was wholly engaged in seeking the pardon of his sins." He goes on by adding that, "the prophets are full of this doctrine, that men are relieved from their evils when they are loosed from the guilt of their iniquities."

James brings forth the example of a man who was definitely not expected to be counted as such: Elijah. He was considered by all in Israel and in the early Church as a superhuman, a super man of faith. One of those who we would consider so highly that it would be unfair to put him at the same level as any of us, "mere mortals." Nonetheless, James tells us that "Elijah was a man just like us." He then brings forth the account of him praying to stop raining, drawn for Jesus teaching (Luke 4:25)—nowhere in the Old Testament will we find him praying for that—and the Lord answered his prayer both to stop the rain and to reinstall it.

What James was trying to communicate to us is that the righteous person is he or she who has confessed their sin and find themselves completely forgiven by God and by those whom they have sinned against (Matthew 6:12—"Forgive us our debts, as we also have forgiven our debtors"). The paraphrase for the end of verse 6 should read this way, "The prayer of those who have a clean slate with God and their brother or sister is powerful and effective." We concur with Kistemaker in this statement, "Prayer offered in faith by a forgiven believer is a powerful and effective means to approach the throne of God."

Again, Kistemaker points out that, "Unconfessed sin blocks the pathway of prayer to God and at the same time is a formidable obstacle in interpersonal relations. That means confess your sins not only to God but also to the persons who have been injured by your sins. Ask them for forgiveness!"

The Apostle Paul wrote to the Galatians, "Carry each other's burdens, and in this way you will fulfill the law of Christ" (Galatians 6:2). This is key in the life of the Church; we must carry each other's burdens. By doing so, we are fulfilling the Great Commandment of Jesus Christ.

It is crucial to observe that the text carries a pastoral weight in many aspects. The calling of the elders, for example, shows that the leadership of the Church must be ready to provide the necessary support in prayer for those who are in need. If the sick member of the congregation cannot be in worship, that member should not feel separated from the flock; instead, by calling the elders, they will be there representing the entire body of Christ. The Church, however, is not made up of elders only; when we are admonished to confess our sins to each other, it implies that we are part of a holy society, the Church of Jesus Christ. In that case, we as a Church must have the attitude of compassion, a society that cares for each other. Nothing is more visible in this area than through the church that prays for each other on a regular basis.

Prayer is also a powerful tool for the missionary call of the Church. We can never underestimate its tremendous impact in the

The Wisdom Of James

life of the Church and also in the Evangelization of the world. I believe that it is because of prayer that the Church becomes a missionary body; as we pray for each other and for other peoples, we enter into a new dimension of ministry that will transform the destiny of many, including ourselves.

On a negative side, a church that does not pray continues to be weak, lacking in spiritual vitality and unable to grow into the stature of Jesus Christ. On a positive side, however, the church that is immersed in prayer is strong, abundant in spiritual vitality, and naturally grows to become like the Lord Jesus, because then it is fulfilling the purpose of God for all of us: to be like his Son (cf. Romans 8:29).

As I conclude this chapter, I want to remind ourselves that prayer is an integral part of the Christian life, be it privately or in the midst of the congregation. It is also a powerful instrument in God's hands if it is offered in faith. The key element that James wants to convey here is that there will be no answered prayer aside of faith. Not only the faith of the elders, but the faith of all those who congregate together; prayer in the church is a mutual part of worship.

Chapter 17

Rescuing the Wayward: The Test of Forgiveness

James 5:19-20

It is enough to discourage any social worker in the slums or in the tenement districts of our cities to see the hopeless condition in which the victims live. Drugs have fastened some with clamps of steel; drink has fired the blood of others; cigarettes have deadened the will of others; and immorality has hurled still others into the pit. They stumble into the rescue halls, "cities of refuge" in our cities. Happy are those who know how to save souls like these who have known better days and who have gone down into the valley of sin and sorrow. (A. T. Robertson, 1912)

We learned in the previous chapter, based on prayer that is offered in faith, that the sick person should call the elders of the church and also that we should confess our sins "before each other so that [we] may be healed." This implies that we know what sins we have committed. Now James is dealing with a different kind of person: someone who is a brother or a sister and have voluntarily departed from the Truth; that is, some one who has left the faith because of sin. Cargal calls them "errant believers."

The Wisdom Of James

There are two ways a person could depart from the Truth: First, because of sins that he or she has committed and by being aware of those sins, that person will leave the fellowship of believers either due to shame or because she or he does not want to repent; or, by being led out of the Truth by some kind of powerful but undetected sin in that person's life, which will lead him or her to abandon, to apostatize from faith completely. It is the command of the Lord, through James, for us to go after those brethren and bring them back to the fold.

I remember a few cases of dear friends who have lost their lives because of sins they have committed and were so ashamed that they never returned to the church. One in particular, I will call "Damian," went bankrupt and along with him the cosigners for his debt. He was a deacon in his church. The shame that came upon him was indeed overwhelming and he could not face the people back in the congregation. He left the church; nobody went after him, except a man of God who was an elder in that church, but also one of his cosigners. That was not enough, Damian continued in a down hill surrender to alcoholism, which was the way he chose to forget his failure. Damian died in a deplorable state of sickness, completely forgotten by his church, but still believing in Jesus Christ. How many people do we know in that situation? It is hard to say, but we see them from time to time.

The king had committed a couple of horrendous sins; his lust, misuse of authority, and poor time management had raised the wrath of God against him. A servant of God came to his rescue, but in the process he had to confront the king: "You are the man!" he said. His courage was the thrust not only of obedience but also of deep love for David (2 Samuel 12). Nathan did to David what James is trying to communicate to us today.

Those persons need to receive the compassion of the church in their lives. We are called to walk the extra mile and reach out for those who have departed from the Truth. It is our duty to rescue them. By going after those who have departed from the Truth, we may be face to face with our own prejudices and reservations against them. It is in times like those that we are before yet another challenge in our faith, the test of forgiveness.

The Rescue Mission

What is at stake here is not the command to evangelize the non-believer, but to rescue the one who has departed from faith. Cargal points out that, "the negative action is clearly that of apostasy, and the positive action of 'restoring' takes place *intramuros* and is not an evangelistic or missionary activity." It is indeed a rescue effort that the Church must be aware of. It is not an easy job. For that reason, the Church is at fault sometimes in doing that. It is easier to put a wayward believer in the inactive roll than to face the situation and try to help him or her. Worse than that, it is easier to just ignore the problem and let it go. One excuse that may be present is that we have so many other options where the believer can shop around: if this particular church does not fit his or her "theology" or "ethic," then the person will certainly find a more accommodating place for worship elsewhere.

Kistemaker approaches the subject with force through the following remark: "Erring members of the church are not necessarily passively waiting to be brought back to the truth. They are not like sheep that have gone astray and are waiting patiently for the shepherd to rescue them. Tactfully reproving a person who is wandering from the truth is one of the most difficult tasks in the work of the church. Numerous pastors, elders, deacons, and church leaders have yielded to the temptation of placing erring members on the inactive list of the church roll. Yet with loving concern, the church must seek out those who are wandering from the truth and urge them to come back."

This difficult aspect of ministry in the church is for every member. James is giving a directive to his readers based on what he was dealing from the very beginning of his Epistle. He ends it rather abruptly but with a clear view of the reality: Anybody in the church can go astray at any time. Therefore, we must be aware of that and be prepared to help them when necessary. One of the most difficult cases of wandering from the truth is when someone rejects the teaching of the Gospel; more to the point, the sound doctrine of the Gospel. At least three incidents in that area come to my mind as I write this paragraph. Although they would serve as "good illustrations" for this chapter, I will rather bow my head and continue to pray for those three dear friends who have left the faith, one of them a former professor of mine. But I remember that in those three cases, several members of the church, both locally and at large, tried their best to rescue them. We still continue to pray for their return to the fold.

I see in this ending of James the urgency of rescuing those who have gone astray. It is something that we as a church and also as individuals ought to do when we are put in a situation that requires it. At the same time, the passage has a significant admonition for me personally: I am not exempt of the possibility of wandering from the faith; I need to always come to the Lord in humbleness to acknowledge that fact. I have been in ministry for over thirty years now and I have seen numerous colleagues of mine succumb to temptations: misappropriation of funds, sexual misconduct, homosexuality, child abuse, heresy, and so forth. Every single time I hear of such bad news, I come to the Lord and pray, asking him to preserve me from falling. In some cases, I am very sad that the church has done so little to help them to overcome their situations and make a U-Turn to God.

It Is Our Corporate Responsibility to Look for the Wayward

Again, James is interpreting the teachings of the Lord Jesus Christ in this letter. Here we clearly see the relationship with Luke 15. There we learn about the three parables of the lost: The Lost Sheep, the Lost Coin, and the Lost Son. All of them are precious teachings for us to keep in mind. It is imperative that we go after those who are lost. Jesus once said that he came to save those who were lost (Luke 19:10 — "For the Son of Man came to seek and to save what was lost").

It was the Lord Jesus also who demonstrated great compassion for Peter, even before he departed from Truth: "Simon, Simon, Satan has asked to sift you as wheat. But I have prayed for you, Simon, that your faith may not fail. And when you have turned back, strengthen your brothers" (Luke 22:32). This is the meaning of "and someone should bring him back." We see later, in the last chapter of the Gospel of John, how the Lord restored Peter into a full relationship with him.

This is part of the "Corporate responsibility Christians have toward another. . . . for spiritual care that is mutual and beneficial" (Kistemaker). We have that responsibility for those who go astray. We learn in Hebrews 3:12-13, "See to it, brothers, that none of you has a sinful, unbelieving heart that turns away from the living God. But encourage one another daily, as long as it is called Today, so that none of you may be hardened by sin's deceitfulness." But also, we are called to bear the burdens of each other (Galatians 6:1). Ezekiel calls our attention to the fact that we are expected to watch for the house of Israel; that is, that we are called to warn those who are away from the Faith, warning the of the danger they are in (Ezekiel 3:16-19). In the case of Ezekiel, we feel the intensity of God's word through the prophet, "Son of man, I have made you a watchman for the house of Israel; so hear the word I speak and give them warning from me. When I say to a wicked man, 'You will surely die,' and you do not warn him or speak out to dissuade him from his evil ways in order to save his life, that wicked man will die for his sin, and I will hold you accountable for his blood. But if you do warn the wicked man and he does not turn form his wickedness or from his evil ways, he will die for his sin; but you will have saved yourself" (Ezekiel 3:17-19).

Who Needs Forgiveness?

The people to be addressed in this passage are the believers who left the Truth. This is not to be understood as being the people who have never heard about the saving grace of the Gospel; no, these are people who once have confessed Jesus Christ as their Savior and now are apostates; people who have left the Church. This is a matter to be dealt as a family matter; not among strangers.

Here we are faced with an important question because the wayward is in great need to be forgiven; but also, we may be in need to receive that forgiveness from them. I remember a church that I served in Brazil where a considerable number of members sided with a pastor who rebelled against the Presbytery and left to form another church in town. As I was still delivering a series of messages in 1 John, the Session of that church realized that they had sinned against the pastor and the group who had left. After meeting with the Women Auxiliary members, I realized that they also felt they had sinned against the group. We set a time that same Sunday afternoon and went to that pastor's home, where the group was meeting, and asked them for forgiveness. The emotions surfaced and they also realized that they had sinned against the church members. Tears and hugs, words of love and reconciliation were present. I was blessed by seeing the group returning to the church and by seeing the pastor being restored by the Presbytery a few weeks later.

There is the shame of sin to be dealt with; the discomfort of the horrendous gulf that sin creates between the sinner and God, but also between the sinner and his or her church. It is our duty to seek them with compassion and to be vulnerable to their needs, if necessary. This is the great example of Jesus Christ, who became sin for our salvation. He who never committed any sin in his life, took upon himself the punishment of the sin of many so they could have life.

It is important to know that many of those who depart from the Truth are no worse than us; thus we should seek them with love and compassion. One thing is necessary to keep in mind, however: It could have been one of us, as I mentioned above. It is now the time we also stop to realize why James dealt with the issue of the tongue in so many different ways (cf. 1:26; 2:6a, 7; 3:1-12; 4:11, 16; 5:9, 12). How we should not judge others, because we may be judged by them as well.

We May Be Saving Someone's Life

The NIV translation renders, "will save him from death." This is a good translation because the word "soul" in the Greek should be better translated by "life," instead of "soul." A person who is saved once will never lose his soul; he or she is saved forever (John 5:24; Ephesians 2:1, 5). But we need to understand that even so, if we depart from the Truth, we may end up dead. There is enough biblical evidence of this sad reality: Paul mentions Hymenaeus and

Alexander, "whom I have handed over to Satan to be taught not to blaspheme" (1 Timothy 1:20). To the man in the Corinthian Church, the "immoral brother," Paul commanded that, "hand this man over to Satan, so that the sinful nature may be destroyed and his spirit saved on the day of the Lord" (1 Corinthians 5:5). Even some who were taken the Lord's Supper unworthily, Paul said that, "that is why many among you are weak and sick, and a number of you have fallen asleep," that is, are dead (1 Corinthians 11: 30). John teaches that "there is a sin unto death" (1 John 5:16).

Jesus Christ taught that, "What good is it for a man to gain the whole world, yet forfeit his soul?" (Mark 8:36). Also in Luke, Jesus affirms the same truth, "What good is it for a man to gain the whole world, and yet lose or forfeit his very self?" This is enough evidence that a person who departs from the Truth, if he or she does not return from his or her sin; that is, convert from sin, will certainly die.

But there is the command from the Lord to rescue those who are perishing: "Rescue those being led away to death; hold back those staggering toward slaughter" (Proverbs 24:11). By walking the extra mile, we will certainly rescue those who have gone astray. This is a life-saving mission for the Church of Jesus Christ. Gordon Poteat points out that this has a lot to do with reconciliation, "[The Church] is the reconciling agent of the kingdom which knows no boundaries; it is the servant of the abundant love of God which is for all peoples." Here we see that he expands the view towards a missionary effort; but, although I believe James is dealing with only the believers, I also think that such application could be used in a broader way.

The Word of God teaches us that love covers a multitude of sins (Proverbs 10:12). As well, Peter also applies that same truth in his first letter, "Above all, love each other deeply, because love covers over a multitude of sins" (1 Peter 4:8). Differently of the teaching in James 5:16, that we should confess our sins to each other, which is a mutual confession; this teaching now thrusts us to confront the sinner with love. It is a very difficult thing to do because not a single person among us is a judge of others; but this act of love, not of judgment, is perhaps the most important way to restore brothers and

The Wisdom Of James

sisters back into a life-saving relationship with themselves, with God, and with the community of faith.

The great blessing out of this is to see the person who once was lost, come back to the Lord in great joy, knowing that the Lord has forgiven him. The Psalmist teaches us that "as far as the east is from the west, so far has he removed our transgressions from us" (Psalm 103:12); and also that "Blessed is he whose transgressions are forgiven, whose sins are covered" (Psalm 32:1). Psalm 85:2, "You forgave the iniquity of your people and covered all their sins." This is the result of such a ministry of forgiveness.

To him, even to the Lord Jesus Christ, be all the Glory
forever and ever!
Amen.

The Epistle of James: Suggested Bibliography

Adamson, James B., *James: The Man and His Message.* Grand Rapids, MI: William B. Eerdmans Publishing Company, 1989.

Brown, Harold O. J., *The Sensate Culture: Western Civilization Between Chaos and Transformation.* Dallas, TX: Word Publishing, 1996.

Calvin, John. *Commentaries on the Catholic Epistles.* Grand Rapids, MI: Baker Book House, reprinted: 1999.

Cargal, Timothy B., *Restoring the Diaspora: Discursive Structure and Purpose in the Epistle of James.* Atlanta, GA: Scholars Press, 1993.

Davids, Peter H., *The Epistle of James: A Commentary on the Greek Text.* (NIGTC). Grand Rapids, MI: William B. Eerdmans Publishing Company, 1982.

Davids, Peter H., *James.* (NIBC). Peabody, MA: Hendrickson Publishers, 1989 [first: 1983].

Guthrie, Donald. *New Testament Introduction.* Downers Grove, IL: InterVarsity Press, 1990.

Guthrie, Donald. *New Testament Theology.* Downers Grove, IL: InterVarsity Press, 1981.

Harrison, Everett F. *Introduction to the New Testament.* Grand Rapids, MI: William B. Eerdmans Publishing Company, 1971.

Hiebert, D. Edmond, *James.* Chicago, IL: Moody Press, 1992.

Kistemaker, Simon J. *Exposition of the Epistle of James and the Epistles of John.* (NTC). Grand Rapids, MI: Baker Book House, 1986.

Ladd, George E., *A Theology of the New Testament.* Revised Edition. Donald A. Hagner, ed. Grand Rapids, MI: William B. Eerdmans Publishing Company, 1993.

Martin, Ralph P. *Word Biblical Commentary — Volume 48 — James.* Waco, TX: Word Books, Publishers, 1988.

Marshall, I. Howard. *New Testament Theology: Many Witnesses, One Gospel.* Downers Grove, IL: InterVarsity Press, 2004.

Maynard-Reid, Pedrito U., *Poverty and Wealth in James.* Maryknoll, NY: Orbis Books, 1987.

Mayor, Joseph B. *The Epistle of James.* Grand Rapids, MI: Kregel Publications, 1990 [first: 1910].

Moo, Douglas J. *The Letter of James: An Introduction and Commentary.* (TNTC). Grand Rapids, MI: William B. Eerdmans Publishing Company, 1985.

Nieboer, James J. *Practical Exposition of the Epistle of James.* Erie, PA: Our Daily Walk Publishers, 1950.

Ogilvie, Lloyd J. *Making Stress Work for You: Ten Proven Principles.* Dallas, TX: Word Publishing, 1985.

Stott, John R. W., *Christian Counter-Culture: The Message of the Sermon on the Mount.* Downers Grove, IL: InterVarsity Press, 1978.

Strauss, Lehman. *James, Your Brother: Studies in the Epistle of James.* Neptune, NJ: Loizeaux Brothers, 1956.

Ehud M. Garcia is a mission theologian, lecturer, pastor and author, born in Araguari, Minas Gerais, Brazil. He is a graduate from the Northern Presbyterian Seminary, Recife, Pernambuco, Brazil (B.Th.'82) and from Fuller Theological Seminary, Pasadena, California (Th.M.'87; Ph.D.'01). He and his wife, Neiva (also born and raised in Brazil), have lived in North America since 1984, serving the Lord as missionaries among several ethnic groups both in Canada and in the United States. Ehud is an ordained minister in the Evangelical Presbyterian Church. As the founder of Diaspora Intercultural Academy, he has also ministered in Brazil, Mozambique, and Russia. Ehud and Neiva have two daughters. They make their home in Lewiston, Idaho.

Diaspora Intercultural Academy is an educational mission organization with the purpose of serving the Church of Jesus Christ through consultations, workshops, formal and non-formal missiological and theological courses. For more details, visit www.diaspora-academy.org.

Contact for conferences, workshops and teaching opportunities:

Ehud M. Garcia, Ph.D.
Diaspora Intercultural Academy
P. O. Box 652
Lewiston, ID 83501 – USA
E-Mail: ehud@diaspora-academy.org

Printed in the United States
133803LV00006B/1-99/P